MULTIFAMILY
INVESTORS WHO
DOMINATE

MULTIFAMILY INVESTORS WHO DOMINATE

AN INSIDE LOOK AT HOW ELITE INVESTORS TRANSACT

BEAU BEERY

AWARD-WINNING MULTIFAMILY BROKER

Multifamily Investors Who Dominate: An Inside Look at How Elite Investors Transact

For information about this title or to order other books and/or electronic media, contact the publisher:

Beau@BeauBeery.com
BRG Realty Ventures LLC
Gainesville, FL
BeauBeery.com

First edition

ISBN Hardcover: 978-1-7358339-0-3
ISBN eBook: 978-1-7358339-1-0
ISBN Audio: 978-1-7358339-2-7

Editing by Wally Bock, Blaine Strickland, and Todd Rainsberger
Copyediting and proofreading by AllMyBest.com
Cover design by Ricky Robbins
Interior layout by DTPerfect.com

Printed in the United States of America

CONTENTS

Elite Investors maximize deposits into their reputation bank account and strive for zero withdrawals.

Elite Investors dominate by systematically building and nurturing a broker network in the markets they master.

Any member of your team, on the acquisition or disposition side, who interacts with investors or brokers is an extension of you and your company brand. Are they costing you deals?

This book is dedicated to my commercial real estate coach, Blaine Strickland, who finally convinced me to write this book for investors, despite the many awesome excuses I gave myself as to why I couldn't or shouldn't. His encouragement, guidance, and experience in commercial real estate, combined with the lessons he learned from becoming a best-selling author in the field, have been incredibly helpful in getting this book written.

FOREWORD

I first met Beau Beery when he contacted my commercial real estate coaching company, The Massimo Group, for our services in early 2014. Since then, I have watched Beau set numerous sales records in his career, predominantly by serving what he refers to in his book as Elite Investors.

I admire Beau for many things, but most of all, he understands that his multifamily investment clients are the heroes in his professional life. It isn't about him. Beau admires their tremendous work ethic, risk tolerance, and intuition, all while balancing staff, partners, investors, lenders, and home life. This perspective allows Beau to focus on creating the best outcomes for each individual client.

Frequently, Beau seeks friendship with his clients. He does not focus just on the transaction at hand. He wants to talk about family and hobbies with them. He touches base with them on their birthdays, anniversaries, and holidays, and he cares about bringing margin to their lives. "Margin" is what I call the happy work/life balance that allows you to meet your career goals of buying more assets while also spending enough time with family, friends, and hobbies.

Multifamily Investors Who Dominate outlines principles of growing an incredible multifamily investment business. Beau has applied these same principles in his own brokerage business and has done exceedingly well—so much so that his coach, Blaine Strickland, calls him "The Freak." When you think about it, investors and brokers are remarkably similar. They are both in competition with their respective peers to win a short supply of opportunities. For investors, the challenge is finding assets to buy and later sell for top dollar. For brokers, finding a qualified investor who wants to transact is the big win. Beau's philosophy is this: the more investors who can transact at an Elite level, the more opportunities and success there will be for everyone involved, including other brokers, investors, attorneys, appraisers, lenders, and all the vendors who service the transaction.

This book will help you buy significantly more deals, sell them for top dollar, and create that precious margin in your life. If these principles work for Elite Investors all over the world, they can work for you. Many Elite Investors started with nothing, or very little, and still grew their investment businesses to epic proportions. Beau has descriptively revealed each of these methods in this book, and I am excited about what they will do for you.

Rod N. Santomassimo
Founder and CEO
The Massimo Group, Inc.

INTRODUCTION

I've been following what I call "Elite Investors" my entire career. These are investors who transact far more deals over a career than their peers. Not all Elite Investors are giant corporations or REITS. Many are small 2–10 person companies that punch way above their bodyweight in terms of deal making. There are plenty of brilliant financial minds out there. What makes Elite Investors elite is that they have figured out the people side of growing an incredible investment business. Elite Investors are masters of human motivation, and you can be too.

You can learn to calculate rates of return all you want, but if you never get a shot at the deal in the first place, what's the point? The mechanics of how to underwrite, negotiate, finance, and manage multifamily assets is far easier than learning how to procure buying opportunities consistently over a long period.

I've been exposed to extreme circumstances in the transacting world of real estate. On the one hand, I've been in situations where I've seen opportunities missed, efforts wasted, and deals crash. On the other hand, I've been at the table with masterful deal makers. They've shown me how their unique approach enables them to see deals and make deals when others couldn't.

I wrote this book to help you become a masterful deal maker. You'll know this book has been valuable to you if you find you are seeing and making more deals than ever. Even if you make just one extra deal in your entire life that makes you six, seven, or eight figures because of one thing you learned from this book, it was worth the read for you and emotionally gratifying for me.

Every real estate investment book I've read is about the nuts and bolts of buying real estate. I wanted to write something different. Other authors talk about how to calculate rates of return, how to test them, how to finance them, how to conduct due diligence, how to manage properties, and so on. I wanted to write about how Elite Investors draw every deal on the market to them, oftentimes before anyone else sees them.

Multifamily investors are the heroes of my world. The entrepreneurial spirit and skill needed to find, underwrite, buy, manage, and eventually sell assets for profit is truly a magnificent dance to witness. You don't learn how to do this overnight. It isn't something based on luck. These investors put millions of dollars into a single investment (unlike buying a few shares of a mutual fund), and have to use all of their skills to reduce risk and make a profit. This is why they are my heroes.

While I was writing this book, people would ask me what it was about. I'd tell them it was the "How to Win Friends and Influence People" methods of growing a giant multifamily empire. This is a people business and always will be. You can learn how to perform the most incredible financial analysis anyone has ever seen, but if you don't know how to bring more deals in the door and then later sell those assets for top dollar, it means nothing.

I started my career in 1999 with Trammell Crow Residential Services (TCRS) in Gainesville, Florida. I was hired as a leasing agent/property manager for a newly constructed 444-unit apartment complex that was just launching the lease-up process. I made between $35,000 and $40,000 per year leasing apartments, handling maintenance calls, resolving tenant disputes, taking deposits, going through leases with tenants, meeting contractors, walking the property, and opening up and locking down the office every day.

Leasing and property managers perform hundreds of tasks each day to run a large, profitable asset. The head property manager and assistant manager were wonderful mentors. I also benefitted from the companywide training program focused on sales and management. I feel very fortunate to have started on the ground floor of a new apartment project. I got to see how they're built, plus layouts and common construction issues, and how a large operator like TCRS was set up corporately, from property managers to regional managers to the national president.

Once I watched the project come together, I was hooked! Guys like Ed Wood (TCRS president at the time) and the rest of his team were like gods to me. They had the experience and guts to create a profitable machine, and they did dozens of these projects all over the country. By the way, the property I started working at in Gainesville in 1999 was worth about $30,000,000 at the time. Today, it is worth north of $60,000,000. This is the business for me!

A large portion of this book is about how to get brokers (and other referral sources) to bring you more deals. Although I am a broker, my goal was *not* to write a book that secretly brainwashes you to bring me or other broker colleagues more deals. If you allow your brain to go down that path as you absorb the techniques I've seen Elite Investors employ, you're going to miss out on the mission of this book.

Multifamily investing is a competition. If you don't agree, you've already lost. In the eight markets I cover, representing nearly the entire northern half of Florida, there are only 1,935 apartment complexes over 10 units, and only 868 that are over 100 units. Those assets are owned by only 960 investors.

Let's assume for a moment an investor buys only conventional apartments (not student or affordable housing). Of those 868 assets that are over 100 units, only 566 are conventional apartments. Of those 566 assets, if the investor buys only the deals that are less than 40 years old but weren't built within the last 5 years, there are only 306 assets. Of those 306 assets, if the investor doesn't want to target assets that have already sold in the last two years because the investor knows it would be difficult to buy the deal for a reasonable price and still add value, then there are only 252 assets left. I could keep drilling down further by eliminating assets that have already refinanced in the last 2 years and thus the defeasance (prepayment penalty) would make selling prohibitive. I could eliminate deals that are owned by long-term funds. I could eliminate deals that have already been fully value-added and so on.

The point is that there are thousands of investors from all over the world, all with seemingly endless amounts of equity and numerous debt sources, who are foaming at the mouth to finance them, and they are all chasing the same 252 assets that you are. So if you think the multifamily investment world isn't one of the most competitive environments on the planet, you're living under a rock. This book reveals how the top of the heap, the Elite Investors, get a first shot at those 252 assets and how they win way more than everyone else.

BROKERS ARE A KEY COMPONENT TO THE STRATEGIES IN THIS BOOK.

Perhaps you've had a bad experience with a broker. Put aside those issues so you don't miss the full value of the methods in this book. Also, when I talk about the methods of getting brokers to bring you more deals, I want you keep in the back of your mind that there are other referral sources than brokers. Many of the methods in this book I describe for outreach to brokers can also be applied to appraisers, title agents, attorneys, third-party property managers, lenders, and so on. Everyone in the industry is a referral source for your next deal.

While a good portion of the book is about how to buy more deals, the book is equally, if not more so, for sellers. Buyers are just sellers in waiting. I typically use the word *investors* to mean both buyers and sellers. I use the word *transact* or *transaction* to be interchangeably meant as buying or selling, depending on the circumstance.

Also, I use the word *broker* throughout the book to describe the salesperson you frequently interact with to buy and sell multifamily deals. Most of the time the people you work with aren't technically brokers. They are salespeople who have their license supervised by a broker. It's an important distinction, but I use broker because nearly everyone reading this book says, "A broker brought me XYZ Apartments." They do not say a "licensed salesperson" brought me the deal. There are times where the investor may indeed be dealing directly with the actual broker. This is typically in franchise or independently owned firms. Brokers own the company, and licensed salespersons are working under the broker.

SPEAKING OF BROKERS, I WROTE THIS FOR YOU TOO.

I want you to feel completely safe in sharing this book with your customers, without feeling like they are going to leave you and come do business with me. You will find that the teachings from Elite Investors are valuable tools you will want your customers to read, learn, and implement in your interactions with them.

At the end of several chapters are suggested Action Steps that can help in implementing the methods of Elite Investors. But remember, consistency is key. Elite Investors consistently perform these methods for incredible results, year after year.

I've included a bonus chapter, entitled, "Family and Friends Come First," that is an important read. We in the multifamily business work extremely hard. It's a grueling 24/7 business, and oftentimes we overwork ourselves. We lose site of the whole reason we work so hard in this business, which is to provide an "elite" life for ourselves and our family. Over the years, Elite Investors have frequently commented to me the importance of having margin in their lives because it actually makes them better at what they do. *Margin* is word for describing the boundaries we set in our work life to allow for hobbies, family, and friends.

Okay. Are you ready for the secrets of how Elite Investors transact? Get ready for your multifamily investment business to explode—in a good way. Let's go!

CHAPTER 1

YOUR REPUTATION—YOUR PERSONAL BRAND—IS THE MOST VALUABLE ASSET YOU HAVE AS AN ELITE INVESTOR

Elite Investors maximize deposits into their reputation bank account and strive for zero withdrawals.

The most important distinction between Elite Investors and everyone else is their fierce protection of their reputation. They are obsessed with building and maintaining a positive reputation any way they can. This chapter is the heart and soul of the book. All chapters that follow are the "how to" of building a reputation in the marketplace that will flood you with more transactions. If you were in the freezing cold and had to use this book to start a fire to stay alive, this is the one chapter you'd want to tear out and save at all costs. You know that in real estate relationships are important. What this really means is that your *reputation* with those relationships is crucial.

As an example, all brokers have several relationships with investors who call them all the time, wanting to buy multifamily assets. When those investors receive a new listing from the broker, they almost never end up buying the deal. The investor's reputation as a friend is probably good. Their reputation as a closer is not good. On the other hand, many brokers have relationships with investors who consistently close more deals than anyone else. The investor's reputation as a friend is probably good. Their reputation as a closer is even better.

The majority of investors don't think about their reputation. The Elite Investors do. They have figured out the secret: there are numerous conversations about you, without your knowing! These are conversations between brokers, investors, attorneys, appraisers, their spouses, their kids, inspectors, surveyors, property managers, and others. And all those people then tell their peers in the industry. If you're doing the things that build your reputation for the positive, there are *dozens* of these conversations. If you're doing the things that build your reputation for the negative, there are *hundreds* of these conversations happening. It is human nature to spread negative gossip at a far greater pace than testimonials. Watch any news station or spend 10 minutes on Facebook, and this will be quickly confirmed for you.

In 2019, Brand Finance announced Porsche as the #1 luxury brand in the world. Elite Investors build a personal brand for themselves in the marketplace. They want to be the "Porsche" to brokers and investors.

Porsche knows that if they build an extremely high-quality, reliable, high-performing vehicle with outstanding customer service, those who interact with them will tell others and those others will tell others. Porsche knows that word of mouth is the strongest brand-building tool in the world. Elite Investors know they need to build a phenomenal personal brand with every interaction in their business. Here's the Brand Finance report that documents the strength of the Porsche brand:

2019	2018	Logo	Name	Country	2019	2018	2019	2018
1 =	1		Porsche		$29,347M	$19,055M	AAA	AAA
2 ^	5		Gucci		$14,662M	$8,594M	AAA	AAA
3 =	3	Cartier	Cartier		$13,642M	$9,805M	AAA-	AAA-
4 v	2	LV	Louis Vuitton		$13,576M	$10,487M	AAA	AAA
5 ^	9	CHANEL	Chanel		$11,480M	$5,884M	AA+	AA+
6 v	4	HERMÈS	Hermès		$10,920M	$9,545M	AAA	AAA
7 v	6		Ferrari		$8,327M	$6,537M	AAA+	AAA+
8 v	7	ROLEX	Rolex		$8,047M	$6,360M	AAA+	AAA
9 v	8	COACH	Coach		$7,544M	$6,189M	AAA-	AAA-
10 ^	16	DIOR	Dior		$6,323M	$4,035M	AAA-	AAA-
11	11		Tiffany &					

I'm a big fan of best-selling author Andy Andrews. His website, AndyAndrews.com, describes what he does best: "He notices the little things that can make a *big* difference in your life." Andy wrote a blog post that has really stuck with me. The post explains what he calls *The Jordan Effect*.

In football, there is a common expression designed to keep players focused on what they can control. They are coached to "compete from the snap to the whistle."

This, of course, means that each player is supposed to give 100% from the time each play starts (when the ball is snapped) to the time the whistle blows and the play is over. It's a concept that can be applied to all sports, and, really, to our lives as well!

But here is something curious I've noticed… while good players truly do give 100% from the snap to the whistle… the very *best* players figure out how to play from the *whistle to the snap*. They are competing at a level where the other guys are unaware there is even a "game" going on!

Have you heard of *The Jordan Effect*?

When Michael Jordan was in his prime with the Chicago Bulls, opposing coaches gave that name—*The Jordan Effect*—to what they were certain was an unfair phenomenon taking place night after night. And the media advanced the notion. Their argument was that the referees were so in awe of Michael that they wouldn't call fouls on him.

As the opposing coaches, their teams, their team's fans, and the media became increasingly obsessed with the idea, someone actually monitored Michael's games for a time and "proved" that The Jordan Effect gave the Bulls at least a five-point advantage in every contest. ESPN announcers often pointed out that the officials were quick to call fouls on opponents who were aggressive with Michael, yet they were hesitant to call fouls on him when he was aggressive with opponents. On Sports Center, we were shown video evidence of the many, many times that Michael was allowed an extra step or two without dribbling and not "called" for traveling.

The Jordan Effect, everyone agreed, was real.

But how did this happen? Was it truly because the officials were awed by his immense talent?

Ahh… no. The Jordan Effect actually had very little to do with Michael's prowess on the court. Michael Jordan had figured out how to play from the whistle to the snap. He was competing during the shoot around before the game. He was competing during TV timeouts. Sometimes, he was even competing back at the hotel before the team ever boarded the bus to the arena. And his opponents had no clue.

If you watched other superstars from that time period, you'll remember how many of them reacted when the refs call them for a foul. Many times—most times—they huffed and puffed and argued with the call. They criticized the officials in the media.

But not Michael Jordan.

Jordan made sure he knew each official by name. So before the game started and the teams were in the arena warming up (or in the lobby of the hotel) he'd talk.

"Hey Steve," he'd say. "How's your son doing? Bobby's in the eighth grade this year, right? I hear he's doing well on the court. You tell Bobby for me that I got cut from my junior high school team. Heck Steve! Your kid is doing better at this stage of his career than I did. You tell him I said to keep it up."

Now, that ref gets to go home to his son and say, "Hey, guess what Michael told me to tell you. Oh, you didn't know? Yes, son… Michael and I are great friends!"

Later, during the game, who do you think gets the benefit of the doubt? Who gets more fouls called… the player griping, complaining, and cussing the official, or the official's buddy—the guy who cares about his son?

The Jordan Effect doesn't only apply to sports. It equally applies to your daily life. That's why a teenager who doesn't make the best grades but knows how to act with respect and good manners will be offered 10 times more opportunities than a kid who makes good grades but doesn't act respectfully and has bad or nonexistent manners.

It is important that we remember to teach our children—and ourselves—that the play is not over when the whistle sounds. Our daily lives don't start at 9 a.m. and end at 5. In order to achieve results beyond the ordinary in every aspect of your life, it's time to figure out how *you* can play from the whistle to the snap.

How do the Elite Investors apply The Jordan Effect to deal making? If the time elapsed from negotiating a contract to closing a deal is the same as the football player's "competing from the snap to the whistle," then Elite Investors build their reputation and brand after closing up until the next deal starts, or "from the whistle to the snap."

Much of this book is about how to transact like Elite Investors, from contract to close, and that is an extremely important component to building your portfolio. **But if you want to compete at a level where the other guys are unaware there is even a "game going on," as Andy describes it, then you have to think differently. Elite Investors win because they focus their game on the time *after* the closing.**

Let me add context to this idea. Elite Investors are extremely selective in their focus because they have only the same 24-hour period to work with as everyone else. As a result, they create criteria for what they will and *won't* work on, and who they will and *won't* work with, in order to maximize their earning efficiency. What they *will* work on is a well-defined asset in a certain market.

As an example, an Elite Investor may deem worthy of their time apartment complexes that:

- Are between 100 and 250 units,
- Are conventional only (conventional means non-student and non-affordable housing),

- Are located in markets that have certain defined demographic and economic guidelines,
- Have an effective age between 1980 and 2005,
- Have a unit mix in which roughly 25% are 1/1s, 50% are 2/2s with little to no 2/1s, and 25% 3/2s,
- Have not already sold or refinanced in the trailing 24 months,
- Are in a C+ location or better that has no chance for the neighborhood to go down in class rank, and
- Offer the ability to add value and boost rents.

They typically won't work on anything that doesn't fit in their defined box. The Elite Investor also has criteria for the type of people they will work with and the type of people they *won't* work with, based 100% on reputation.

In my early 20s I would take on any property listing from any investor. As a commission-based salesperson, I had to put food on the table. You may recognize this same pattern in your own career. So I'd work on poorly located, dilapidated, overpriced assets. I'd work with investors who I knew were sleazy, conniving, hot tempered, or unrealistic, and as a young broker I didn't care. My time had little value. I wasn't flooded with business to the point that I needed to start making better choices on the quality of the assets or people with whom I worked. I derived a certain satisfaction from doing difficult deals with difficult people because I felt the investment world would look at me and say, "Man, that guy is really good at what he does if he could sell that property to that guy."

I now know that working with people whose reputation is poor in the marketplace usually leaves a stain behind. No matter how well I handled a transaction when working with a disreputable investor, it still left a bad taste in the mouths of everyone involved. I quickly learned that, no matter the size of the fee I might earn, working with professionals who aren't respected in the market isn't worth staining my personal brand.

As an investor, remember how extremely important your reputation is and how every move you make, every decision you make, is seen by others involved and quietly talked about with others. This is the cornerstone of why Elite Investors win so much more business than everyone else.

An investor I know acquired five apartment complexes totaling 700 units from different sellers over a two-year period. I wasn't involved in any of the deals as a listing or selling agent, but I knew most of the sellers and the brokers involved in the deals.

Since I vigorously research each sale, I chatted with the sellers and brokers about these transactions. They all had negative things to say about this buyer on every transaction. He re-traded pricing for no justifiable reason. He asked for credits on items that were extremely minor. He'd be consistently rude and generally difficult. He always tried to make the broker cut the commission. This investor had decided to use the bully approach to investing.

I entered all of this information into my CRM (Customer Relationship Management) database, and then called the investor to introduce myself. I like to call new players in the market to congratulate them and learn about their acquisition criteria.

He gave me his purchase criteria and talked about how great a buyer he is, that he closes quickly, never re-trades, and has plenty of capital. Then he told me all the bad things done to him by the sellers and brokers. I recorded these notes, too. The bottom line is, this is an investor I was choosing to avoid if possible because five different sellers and brokers had something negative to say about him and the way he conducted each deal.

Five years later, I still can't bring myself to include him on a deal. A missed opportunity for me? Maybe. A missed opportunity for him? Definitely.

I've sold thousands of units over the last five years that would have met his specific buying criteria, and he didn't get a look at any of them. Think about the millions of dollars in potential profits he has missed out on from not seeing my listings and the listings of all the other brokers in the markets.

This investor will eventually make money selling his assets, but his pipeline of future acquisitions will always be a struggle because other brokers and investors don't want to work with him. In the end, this investor's reputation has harmed him, and it represents the exact opposite of how Elite Investors act.

ELITE INVESTORS UNDERSTAND THE WORST PART OF A BAD REPUTATION IS THAT THE AMOUNT OF THE LOSS IS UNKNOWN AND INCALCULABLE.

Elite Investors make every decision with their reputation in mind. They choose the path that is the right thing to do, even when it costs them money, because making the wrong decision costs them far more over their career.

The bad-reputation investor in my story above has no idea how much money he loses every day because of his reputation. I'm one of roughly 60 multifamily brokers in the region I cover. How many of the other 59 brokers think twice about showing him anything?

The most successful multifamily brokers in the country place more value on working with high-quality-reputation investors than on the size of the fee. Reputation can be extremely powerful in a good way and catastrophic in a bad way. You can't see it. You can't touch it. But its presence shows up everywhere you go, before you even get there. Like Michael Jordan, you've won (or, perhaps, lost) the game before you even show up on the court.

I know many investors reading this book don't have the opportunity to work with an Elite Investor in a brokerage role like I do, so I'll try to describe what attracts me and other brokers to Elite Investors. Getting to know an Elite Investor is like meeting your spouse for the first time. I remember very well the first real date I had with my wife back in 1998. After the date, I walked into my apartment. My roommate said I looked like I'd seen a ghost because I was really white and looked dazed and confused. I told him, "I think I've met my wife." I just knew she was special. I wanted to be around her all the time. I wanted to do things for her. I wanted to impress her.

Working with Elite Investors is very similar. As a broker, I can't wait to do another deal with them. I want to hang out with them as a friend. I want to do things for them that have nothing to do with a transaction. I desperately want to impress them. They have this way about them that I respect because they respect me and others. They make others feel valued. They always do what they say they are going to do in a transaction. While you may not have the opportunity to broker a deal with an Elite Investor, I do hope you will have the privilege of meeting and transacting with them as a principal in the future. And I really hope you become one. They are extremely rare but very easy to identify, once you've done one deal with them.

Elite Investors are by no means perfect! They make mistakes like everyone else, but the way they handle them actually builds their reputation. Here's an example. I was part of a small transaction in which I was the listing broker. An Elite Investor won the deal and went to contract as the buyer. It was a relatively smooth transaction except for one tiny issue. The letter of intent (LOI) from the buyer had called for the buyer to pay for title insurance. No one remembers exactly how the situation evolved, but everyone signed a purchase and sale agreement calling for the seller to pay for title insurance.

In a rare moment of greed, this otherwise Elite Investor mandated that seller pay title insurance because that is what everyone agreed to in the binding contract. I must say I was shocked that an Elite Investor would make an issue of such a tiny amount compared to the whole deal. This really ticked off the seller, but he had to agree. No other hiccups occurred, and the deal closed. For several weeks after the closing, the seller would bring up that title issue and complain how petty and ridiculous it was that the buyer had acted that way. It was obvious the seller would never transact with that buyer again. About six weeks later, I got a call from the seller and this is how I remember it. We'll call the Elite Investor "George":

Seller: You'll never believe this, but George called me last week to apologize for the title issue during our transaction.

Me: Oh, wow, that's really classy.

Seller: Yeah, it was. George said he'd had a terrible lapse of judgment and was monumentally embarrassed. He then sent me a check for the title insurance! I was floored.

Me: That is so awesome to hear, and it isn't too surprising to me. What he did was so uncharacteristic of him that I'm sure it was eating him alive.

Seller: Well, I was really impressed. George was actually a great buyer, and I'd certainly do business with him in the future.

I called George and complimented him for his refreshing integrity. This is what it means to transact at an elite level.

If you want to be an Elite Investor, *protect your reputation!*

Elite Investors...	Average Investors...
Fiercely protect their reputation.	Rarely consider their reputation.
Compete from the "whistle to the snap" *and* the "snap to the whistle."	Marginally compete from the "snap to the whistle."
Stick to strict acquisition criteria.	Veer from criteria due to impatient capital and/or FOMO (Fear of Missing Out)
Carefully select people with whom they do business, hire, and spend personal time.	Allow shortsightedness and desperation for growth to justify their transactions in business, staffing, and friendships that drag down their reputation.
Treat every party and situation with respect and professionalism in order to close the deal and protect their outstanding reputation.	Want to win every disagreement at all costs, without leaving a dime on the table. Give no consideration to what anyone thinks of them after closing (if a closing even occurs).
Develop a long-term pipeline of opportunities.	Focus solely on winning the deal in front of them, with no long-term consideration of their deal pipeline.
Are people others like to be around and look forward to speaking with, doing deals with, and working for. Brokers and investors seek them out first.	Are usually considered after Elite Investors have been shown the investment opportunity. Brokers don't think first about them.
Always right their wrongs in the rare moments of poor judgment.	Never admit they are wrong or attempt to right the wrong.

Action Steps:

- Visit AndyAndrews.com. Operating in real estate with the principles Andy teaches will set you far apart from the competition. Your biggest problem in business will be hiring enough quality staff to keep up with all your buying and selling. While on the site, do the following:
  - Subscribe to his Podcast.
  - Buy and read the book, *The Bottom of the Pool* (located on the Store page). This book uses great storytelling that can be applied to the way Elite Investors operate in the multifamily business.
  - Spend time watching his videos.
  - As you listen, read, and watch the different material from Andy Andrews, think about how you can apply these principles in your investment business. Elite Investors have mastered these principles. For most of us, it isn't natural and requires practice.
  - Reread "The Jordan Effect" blog and think how Michael Jordan's methods of treating others could create the extra edge in the multifamily arena.
- Read the book *Mr. Shmooze* by Richard Abraham, purportedly a book about a real-life commercial real estate broker who operates his business much like Elite Investors do.
- Study the chart located earlier in this chapter, of the Top 10 brands in the world, and ask yourself how you feel about each of those brands. Why do you think the world puts their reputations on a pedestal? Visit their social media pages and watch how customers talk about them. None of these brands reach this level without making constant deposits in their reputation bank account with

their customers, suppliers, retailers, partners, staff, and so on. They do the right thing, every time, regardless of money.

- Are there transactions or interactions in the past, now that you look back, that you could have handled differently? Perhaps there were brokers, investors, attorneys, appraisers, vendors, or others with whom you had interactions that didn't end on a good note? Was the cost of the decision at that time worth it in the end? Did those interactions really have any substantial effect on your ROI in the end? Consider reaching back out to those professionals and talk to them. A sincere apology, as hard as it is, could reap tremendous benefits in the future. It is human nature to hold grudges, and simple apologies can free up the most ill of feelings toward others. You may be able to end years of bad word of mouth about you that these people may be spreading.

- If you have a situation that needs remedying, you might consider how Johnson & Johnson came out of a crisis (in which people died) as a hero. Google "Tylenol made a hero of Johnson & Johnson: The recall that started them all," an article written by Judith Rehak of *International Herald Tribune*.

We've now established how critical your reputation is in the markets you operate in, and how reputation is the number one difference between Elite Investors and everyone else. Beginning in the next chapter, we'll discuss how Elite Investors use that positive reputation to have every deal in the market brought to them.

CHAPTER 2

ELITE INVESTORS DON'T SOURCE DEALS, DEALS COME TO THEM

Elite Investors dominate by systematically building and nurturing a broker network in the markets they master.

Here's an important statistic you should know. Our firm reviewed 350 randomly selected multifamily-sale transactions from January 2015 through the 1st quarter of 2020, which represented 31% of all transactions in that period for the northern half of Florida, and calculated that 92.55% of the sales were procured by a broker! If that number surprises you, it shouldn't. While this statistic may differ by region, the fact remains that the majority of multifamily closings are procured by a broker.

LET'S THINK ABOUT IT.

Investors have many competing interests as they try to close a deal. They are constantly faced with the challenge of having to do the following:

- Raise equity.
- Find and negotiate debt sources.
- Hire, train, and maintain the right property managers, leasing agents, maintenance staff, accountants, attorneys, and acquisition and disposition team members.
- Communicate with investors.
- Underwrite deals.
- Plan for the short and long term.
- Find contractors and negotiate and manage rehabs.

The list goes on and on. It is impossible for an investor, even an Elite Investor, to do all these things *and* be good at sourcing new deals and selling them for top dollar.

Multifamily brokers spend every waking second of their days, and many of their nights and weekends, doing two things: listing and selling apartment complexes. The majority of a broker's time is spent concentrating on how to find apartment deals to sell.

Multifamily brokers in the markets I cover beat investors to the punch (the "punch" being finding assets for sale) 92.55% of the time. Brokers have mastered the technique of figuring out which assets are going to sell next. Elite Investors have figured out that if they concentrate on mastering their relationships with brokers, instead of trying to buy and sell deals themselves, they will be able to concentrate on other important things in their business that maximize their overall performance and profitability.

Some investors have taken this approach to the extreme, hiring a multifamily broker to come on staff and paying them a salary plus bonuses to find them deals. This typically doesn't produce nearly the same results because the motivations of a salaried salesperson and a commissioned broker who must sell to put food on the table are starkly different.

A few Elite Investors I've studied have large organizations, but most of them are small- to mid-size companies run by 1–2 people with fewer than a dozen staff members. Getting to know them over the years, studying all their deals, and being a part of several of those deals along the way, I found one fact stood out: *a broker was involved in every single deal.* They sold every one of their assets using a broker; and every deal they bought had been brought to them by a broker, and typically they were among the first to see it.

The Elite Investors I've studied concentrate on broker relationship building. None of the principals or their transactional staff spend time making calls themselves directly to owners to try to find that needle in a haystack. They are all too busy underwriting deals that brokers brought to them. There is no time to try to find a deal themselves. It makes no sense trying to compete against full-time brokers with decades of experience. Elite Investors have figured out that relying on brokers to do their buying and selling is like having dozens of extremely well-qualified staff members, working for free, who eagerly want to help them grow their business.

It makes far more sense to direct your time and efforts into building relationships with the brokers in your market than it does spending time trying to find, buy, and sell assets yourself.

Here is a plan I developed after observing Elite Investors for over 20 years. No Elite Investor I know implements all these strategies in the exact way I describe. Each of them carries out these steps in their own style. Do you have to implement every strategy below, exactly as I have written, to become an Elite Investor? No, but I can tell you that those who do follow this plan will greatly increase the probability of seeing far more deals brought to them for acquisition than the average investor who is not following this plan. I'm giving you the plan because the majority of humans aren't natural relationship builders.

THE PLAN BELOW ISN'T EASY, BUT IT PRODUCES CONSISTENT SUCCESS FOR ELITE INVESTORS.

First, consider calling a meeting with every partner, equity source, or staff member who has direct contact with a broker. Make sure they're convinced that one of the keys to transacting like an Elite Investor is building strong relationships with every multifamily broker in your markets.

Then, buy a CRM (Customer Relationship Management) software license for each of the folks on your team who interact with brokers (including and especially the principal investors). I don't recommend Microsoft Excel or Outlook to carry out this program. I'm asking you to think like a salesperson because that's what you are at this point. Elite Investors are selling themselves—their brand and reputation—to brokers, lenders, attorneys, appraisers, etc., to grow relationships that pay financial dividends.

All great salespeople manage their businesses using a CRM. There are many CRMs out there, and using the same ones that commercial real estate brokers use can work well for investors. Commercial real estate CRMs have contact data cards, property data cards, and vendor data cards. You can schedule events, track history, take notes, upload pictures, track rental and sale comps, and send emails, and the list goes on. My favorite is RealNex. Check my website BeauBeery.com for a special offering from RealNex. Other popular CRMs used by investors and brokers can be found at the end of this chapter.

Everyone should be on the same system and contribute to the same records within the CRM. It is helpful to know if your partner just called a certain broker and what was discussed. The history of conversations is important so you can look back at every touch and can reference those discussions in future interactions. Always seek to have a next event scheduled for every person.

Now that you have the CRM, master how it works. Have the CRM company train your people. Watch videos about the software, play with it, and become extremely comfortable with it. Ultimately, the CRM should be a seamless tool for everyone on the team.

Next, add every single multifamily broker in all of your markets into your CRM. *All of them*—even the ones you've never met or don't like. These will range from full-time multifamily specialists to commercial brokers who may be generalists but occasionally list a multifamily property. Be sure to enter at least the following information per contact:

- Full contact information (including phone, email, and mailing address)
- A picture of them (all CRMs have this ability) uploaded from LinkedIn, Facebook, or their company website
- Their social media accounts
- Business website
- Notes about them (family or kids' names, sports, hobbies, where they went to school, spouses, etc.)
- Birthdays, anniversaries, holidays (keep in mind different religions), kids' birthdays, etc.
- Anything else you or your staff can learn about them over time

Have one of your staff scour the internet for anything about each broker. You can usually find out a lot about them from social media. Find articles they were in, where they went to school, previous jobs, awards they've won, etc. This "notes" section will be built upon year after year as you continue to learn more about them. Elite Investors and their staff are awesome at this.

Next, rank each multifamily broker A, B, or C, just like you would an apartment complex. You are ranking each broker in order to be the most efficient with your time in building your relationship with them. You'll spend more time building relationships with higher ranking brokers. An "A" is the top ranking, "B" is next best, and "C" not surprisingly is less than B. What goes in to a ranking? It is subjective but based on which broker can be the most productive for you. A productive broker tends to be strong with sales volume, has good experience, can source you deals, and has a solid reputation in the marketplace.

Rank A—productive, and I like this person
Rank B—productive, but I don't like this person as much
Rank C—not as productive

Now that you've ranked each broker, create a contact schedule for each broker throughout the year and enter that schedule in your CRM. You and your staff can be more aggressive in your "touches," but following is a suggested *minimum* schedule I've experienced that Elite Investors tend to abide by, in order for them to be most effective:

- Rank A's—Meet in person 2–4 times per year, talk on phone at least every 30–60 days.
- Rank B's—Meet in person 1–2 times per year, talk on phone at least every 90–120 days.
- Rank C's—Meet in person for the first introductory time, talk on phone every 180 days.

- Add all brokers to your once-a-month "drip marketing" campaign of emails and mailings. A drip marketing campaign for Elite Investors involves sending out periodic emails, mailings, and social media messages about the market, their own operations, or other industry-related information.

A "touch" is really any form of communication… meet in person, Zoom, phone call, email, or mailing. The communication that has the highest ROI (return on investment) is meeting in person. No matter what excuse is entering your head right now as to why meeting with brokers (or anyone) is inefficient or that you know of better ways, please reconsider. Can you have a meaningful conversation on the phone in 5 minutes? Yes. Is it more impactful than the 90 minutes it takes to drive somewhere and do lunch, or the broker stops by your office? No. Phone calls are efficient and effective. They just aren't as effective as meetings.

A more powerful bond is created when two people meet. Elite Investors understand meeting is the best way to achieve the Jordan Effect with their investing. Meeting in the flesh is a totally different experience. It makes the person real. Their face is burned into your brain. You see pictures on their walls. You talk about things you wouldn't have over the phone. You shake hands or do fist/elbow bumps. You smile more, and the list goes on. If you're more than a drive away, then be more strategic about how you get meetings.

I know several Elite Investors who schedule a number of meetings at an annual conference, like the National Multifamily Housing Council (NMHC) conference. The next time you know you're going to be touring a market, or viewing a property even if it's listed by a different broker, make it a point to meet with other brokers in that market. Stay an extra day if needed. I know Elite Investors who live in destination markets like Orlando, Florida, or New York, California, Boston, or parts of Texas, and they will remind brokers that if their family ever vacations to their town, they'd love to meet them.

Zoom calls can be effective in between in-person meetings. I'm writing this book amidst a global pandemic, which forces me to use Zoom every day. Meetings are trickier at the moment but are still completely possible with the right precautions. Even under those conditions, an in-person meeting is preferred. Elite Investors meet with brokers and other important referral sources as a part of their growth strategies. I encourage you to be aggressive in setting up these meetings. If the brokers aren't calling you to meet, then call them. They spend the majority of their time trying to get meetings (and are oftentimes rejected), so to be asked to a meeting earns big points. The Elite Investors I know call me many times a year to set up meetings at conferences, or when they are in town touring.

I know a few Elite Investors who put together private events specifically to engage with brokers. I was recently invited to a student housing developer's privately owned ranch for a weekend to go quail hunting, eat amazing food prepared by a private chef, go horseback riding, and have drinks around the fire with him and other members of the company. After a weekend like that, who do you think is among my first phone calls for a new development site listing I get?

When possible, also try to meet the broker's support staff and partners. Many brokers have an assistant, analyst, marketing person, junior broker, and/or another partner. Make it a point to meet all of them at least once. If you hit it off with the staff too, you have the support of other team members who sing your praises in your absence.

Virtual meetings can be very productive, even as a supplement to in-person meetings. One benefit to virtual meetings over in-person meetings is it's easier to "screen-share," the act of showing the investor exactly what's on your computer screen. I know you can show what's on your computer screen in a live meeting, but it is awkward to sit really close to each other, and the other person can see everything on your desktop. In a virtual meeting you can control exactly what they see. When on camera, be yourself. When people feel like they can be themselves on camera or in front of someone, there is another level of connection. I'm not saying you can come in from mowing the lawn with your shirt off, or you just woke up and still have sleep in your eyes, but you get the point. Don't pass up this simple but highly effective means of communication that will drive closer bonds, which will in turn net you more deals.

Beyond meeting in person or a virtual meeting, talking on the phone is the next best thing. Phone calls don't need to be—and they shouldn't be—30+ minute conversations every time. In the beginning of the relationship, it is important to have a few minutes at the beginning of the call to discuss personal lives, hobbies, what you did on the weekend, kids, etc. You want to get to know the broker, so these calls may be a little longer than 5 minutes in the beginning. As the two of you develop a bond, the *get to know you* phase can be less and the business part of the call more. Your goal doesn't necessarily need to be getting to a point where your calls are less than 5 minutes. Each person and relationship is different. Elite Investors reach out to brokers so frequently that each call is typically very short because the relationship is so strong.

Emails as your main point of communication is a no-go. Emails should only be used as a "connector" between meetings and phone calls. You can't replace meetings and phone calls with emails. Elite Investors aren't elite because they got awesome at sending emails. Emails are great to communicate quick info in between meetings and calls and are excellent at sending rich information of value and to stay top of mind.

I suggest sending something of high value to brokers once per month. This could be something industry related or something personal to them. Brokers really appreciate learning about a property you just bought or sold and all the financial metrics because it gives them accurate comparable sale information. If you've done a good job of getting to know the broker, then send something you saw about their hobby. If you know a broker is big into cars, maybe you found a really interesting article on a vehicle they love. If you know the broker will be vacationing in New York, you send them the menu of a couple restaurants you like. The point is please don't use emails as your only form of communication—but when you send them, make them count.

The "touch" schedule I have outlined above are the minimums. The more meetings, calls, and emails you convey (assuming they are meaningful touches and not just fluff), the better. You want to occupy the top of mind in the broker's head. Brokers spend most of their lives trying to build relationships with investors. They are constantly being told "No," being delayed, or being blown off. To have an investor initiate contact and show genuine interest in them is so out of the ordinary and so incredibly refreshing, that the magnification of your efforts is enormous. Trust me.

ELITE INVESTORS HAVE OPPORTUNITIES SHOWERED UPON THEM. THEY DON'T NEED TO SCOUR THE MARKET FOR OPPORTUNITIES.

You may roll your eyes at my next piece of advice, but it's really effective. Attempt to be on the email and mailing list of all the brokers in your markets. Have them add you or go to their websites and subscribe and connect on all their social media accounts. You could even create a separate email account for this communication. You want to get their new listings, marketing reports, closing announcements, etc. I know the natural instinct is to unsubscribe because we all get so many emails, but the point is to develop as close a relationship as you can with those who are responsible for 92.55% of all deals in the multifamily sector.

Having their material sent to you via email and mail gives you a super easy topic to call or email them about. Think about it. If you just sent an email out to your investors about a property you just put under contract and one of the investors called you to compliment you on how great a job you're doing, how would that make you feel? Let's say you send the message that your new construction asset leased up a month ahead of time and a broker emailed you that he/she hasn't seen that kind of leasing in a long time. Makes you feel pretty good, right? You'd remember that person's saying that for a long time. It took that broker 20 seconds to type that reply. You don't get these simple opportunities to create a little bond if you aren't on their distribution lists and social media accounts.

I know an Elite Investor in central Florida who is awesome on social media in responding to broker posts about deals closed, new listings, articles they've written or shared, new hires, or what fun they had on the weekend. For 15 minutes a day, get on LinkedIn, Twitter, Facebook, YouTube, Instagram, etc., and like and comment. You can set up these accounts to show you posts by certain people first so you don't have to scroll through hundreds of other posts to see the ones you want. In the early stages of befriending brokers you don't know, I'd start with LinkedIn, Twitter, and YouTube. Once you've reached a comfortable point in the friendship, friend them on Facebook.

Save all these brokers and other referral sources in your cell phone so you know when they are calling. It also feels good to the other person calling when you answer with "Hey Beau, always good to hear from you." It starts off the call with a great tone when you know who is calling.

Set up Google Alerts for every broker and referral source. When you get a notification from Google on a broker, you can click on it and see what it says. Then, you can shoot that link to the broker and comment on it. They will be really impressed. For instance, if some magazine did an article on them, or a sale they did, simply forward that article to them and tell them you read it and then congratulate them. If you don't know what a Google Alert is or how to set it up, just Google it!

You *must* add every broker and referral source to your own *drip marketing* campaign. You should be telling the world about yourself and your accomplishments, on a scheduled basis. I suggest an email once per month and then a separate piece by snail mail 4–12 times per year. The drip could be about a property you just bought, the metrics, an employee or partner you gained, a market report, a closing, philanthropy your company is involved in, or a holiday card. Don't think of drip marketing as "look how great I am." That isn't the point. Some Elite Investors have a drip marketing campaign that is sent to brokers or referral sources. By adding brokers to your drip marketing campaign, it shows them that you are a player who is very active and serious about transacting, and with a reputation for winning.

THE FINAL SUGGESTION I HAVE FOR BUILDING BONDS WITH BROKERS AND REFERRAL SOURCES IS RESERVED FOR THE ELITE OF THE ELITE.

This is next-level kind of stuff. Organize one broker/referral-source appreciation event or reward per year. This is reserved only for the most productive relationships for the time period. It might be for the five brokers who bought and/or helped sell deals for you that year. Salespeople love to hit goals and be part of something exclusive. Heck, who doesn't like to be part of something exclusive that they earned? If there are 60 brokers in your market, and 5 went to the event because they were the most productive, that word spreads to the other 55 and they want to be part of that group next year. If you are cultivating relationships with all 60 agents, then all 60 agents will want to be among those who come.

Let's talk about the event. First, consider geography and the size of your operation. The event could be a destination event where they come to you, or you could meet them somewhere. It would need to be a good-enough event for some brokers to potentially want to fly somewhere. That doesn't eliminate the event; it just means it would need to be good enough to make it worth taking a day or two off from their own lives to go somewhere. The event could be a hunting day or weekend, a fishing trip, or a NASCAR driving day.

As an alternative, maybe you send each broker something of meaningful value. This could be personal to them or it could be generic to all of them if it were something desirable enough. Doing something special for them is preferred. That way the reward can be based on the transaction value you had with them. Obviously, if one broker brought you two $8 million deals, it wouldn't make much sense to give them the same-value reward as the person who did $30 million in volume with you. Examples may be a weekend trip to a resort near them, a fishing trip, an exotic car rental for a year, a Disney weekend if they have children, or a college or professional sporting event—the list goes on. To become an expert at gifting and for ideas, I suggest reading the book, "Gift-ology" by John Ruhlin. He is the master.

For all events, experiences, or rewards, if there is ever a chance to take into consideration their spouses and kids, that is super powerful. You don't have to include this all the time, because some folks like the time away from family, but consider mixing it in every few years. When you can bond with their families, and the family truly enjoys your event, it is hugely powerful.

An Elite Investor...	An Average Investor...
Focuses on referral source relationships (brokers) to grow their portfolio.	Spends more time trying to procure a deal directly with an owner.
Always works with brokers when selling to ensure maximum value and ideal terms.	Occasionally tries to save on broker fees by doing a deal directly with a buyer.
Uses a companywide CRM to track history and schedule relationship building.	Uses an outdated system or has no method to actively track and schedule relationship building.
Actively and consistently seeks out relationships with every broker in the market, regardless of productivity or likeability.	Inconsistently reaches out to only a few brokers in the area.
Gets to know every broker personally, thus building a stronger, more meaningful bond that goes beyond real estate.	Doesn't build bonds with brokers and keeps things strictly business.

An Elite Investor...	An Average Investor...
Uses a broker ranking system that maximizes their time and output with each broker.	Has no system for evaluating their time and output efforts with brokers.
Puts top priority on meetings and calls to build strong broker relationships.	Relies overwhelmingly on emails to brokers with an occasional phone call.
Looks for opportunities to communicate and add value to brokers so they stay top of mind.	Views brokers as an annoyance and underestimates the importance of their role in growing their portfolio.
Has a strong drip-marketing program.	Has no drip-marketing program.
Creates annual appreciation events or awards to thank those who helped grow their business.	Offers no incentive to keep referral sources motivated to bring them more opportunities.

Action Steps:

- Call a meeting with all team members involved in the purchase and sale of apartment deals in your company. Work through the idea that time is far better spent building successful broker relationships than trying to find a needle-in-the-haystack deal directly from a seller.

- For each team member, consider purchasing, installing, and religiously using a CRM (Customer Relationship Management) system. Become a master at how the CRM works. Other CRMs besides RealNex to consider at the time of this writing are ClientLook, Apto, Rethink, Salesforce, Hubspot, Buildout, and AscendixRE, to name a few.

- Include in your CRM every multifamily agent in the market(s) you work.

- Rank each multifamily agent in your CRM as an A, B, or C agent.

- Create recurring action dates in your CRM with each agent, based on their ranking:
  - Rank A's—Meet 2–4 times per year and talk on phone at least every 30–60 days.
  - Rank B's—Meet 1–2 times per year and talk on phone every 90–120 days.
  - Rank C's—Meet for the first introductory time but then talk by phone every 180 days.
  - Note: If live meetings are impossible, replace with a Zoom or similar meeting.
- Be sure to sign up for every agent newsletter, market report, market survey, new-listing email blast, etc.
- Connect with the agent on LinkedIn and Twitter and "follow" them to see and comment on their actions. If they have a business YouTube channel, subscribe. Make it a point to interact in these channels at least once per week and preferably 2–3 times per week.
- When the relationship has reached a comfortable level, connect with them on more personal platforms like Facebook and Instagram.
- Save the agent in your cell phone so you know when they are calling.
- Make it a point to meet (by phone or in person) their assistant and/ or other partners on the team.
- Find out their birthdays and anniversaries and enter them in your CRM so you can touch base with them.
- Learn their religion and enter major religious dates in your CRM so you can communicate with them ahead of time.
- Set up Google Alerts for their name, their partners' names, and their company to learn when articles including them come out.

- Add them to your own drip marketing program of newsletters, emails, mailings, etc. about closings you've done, partners you're working with, investors you've gained, new hires, etc.
- Organize at least one major broker appreciation event or reward per year. Ask brokers about events or rewards they've received in the past that have stuck out in their mind. Get it on the calendar, plan it, execute it, and repeat *every* year. Consider hiring an event planner; they are well worth the cost.
- Read *Gift-ology* by John Ruhlin.

We've established that brokers are responsible for the vast majority of all closings in the market, and we've identified who they are, how to track them, how often Elite Investors communicate with them, and how Elite Investors establish rapport with them beyond the transaction. In the next chapter, we'll dive in to how some Elite investors make sure they and their whole team are doing all the right things to maintain a huge pipeline of opportunities flowing their way from those brokers and other potential referral sources in the market.

CHAPTER 3

YOUR PARTNERS AND STAFF ARE AN EXTENSION OF YOUR BRAND

Any member of your team, on the acquisition or disposition
side, who interacts with investors or brokers is an
extension of you and your company brand.
Are they costing you deals?

This chapter could make you feel uncomfortable but, believe me, it is critical. If you can become excellent at building your brand and befriending brokers to grow your business, then you naturally understand that every member of your company must practice these concepts as well. Everyone must be fully committed to treating everyone outside the organization with the highest caliber of professionalism and respect. Just one member of a team can hurt your reputation and keep you from seeing more deals or selling for top dollar. The larger your organization is, the harder it is to recognize those who might be holding you back. Before we look at how you make sure you have the right approach on the team, let's first look at how you can measure success.

THE MEASUREMENT OF YOUR REPUTATION IN THE MULTIFAMILY DEAL-MAKING MARKETPLACE IS WHAT I CALL THE "LOVE FACTOR."

The Love Factor is calculated as follows:

$$\frac{\text{Total number of properties that were brought to you directly by a broker (or another referral source), whether on or off the market}}{\text{Total number of all closings in those same markets}} \times 100 = \text{Love Factor \%}$$

For example, if you buy conventional apartment complexes over 100 units in Jacksonville, Orlando, and Gainesville only, and I showed you that in 2019 there were 98 apartment complexes that closed in that category, then ideally you would find that all of those complexes were presented to you when they were for sale. If so, your Love Factor would be 100%. If you looked at that list of 98 closings and had seen only 10 of them, then your Love Factor is only 10.2% (10 divided by 98). Believe it or not, Elite Investors have a Love Factor of at least 80%, though they are in constant pursuit of 100%.

Some Elite Investors take this concept a step further. They measure the number of closings they conducted against the number of properties that traded in the market, or against the number of properties that were presented to them. This can be a valuable second metric, but for the moment, I want to focus on just the number of "at bats" you got—which is your Love Factor. If you have a high Love Factor every year, the chances are extremely high that it is because you've gotten really good at closing deals you put under contract. If you weren't good at closing deals, you wouldn't be seeing many deals in the first place. They go hand in hand, which is why the Love Factor is so important.

Now that you know what a high Love Factor is, you need to track it. The simplest way is to use a spreadsheet like the one on page 36. I suggest making the spreadsheet accessible to everyone on your team, perhaps through Google Docs, so that anyone can make additions to it. When a broker sends you or a team member a property for sale, it is immediately logged on the spreadsheet. You can track many details about the opportunity, but it starts with keeping track of the total number of opportunities seen by the team. I call this simply the Love Factor spreadsheet; see next page.

Using the same spreadsheet, but adding a second tab, track every closing that fits your criteria in the market. I call this the Market Closing Tracker. (See page 37.) I strongly suggest that you *not* do this internally. Instead, lean on those brokers who have historically produced strong analytics on the market to produce this information for you. It takes tremendous time and energy to track every closing, and good brokers will have the information. This is the perfect topic for the regularly scheduled call you learned about in Chapter 2. If you choose to track this information yourself, page 37 provides a sample spreadsheet. You'll be able to calculate how many total deals occurred and then compare that total to the ones you've seen on the Love Factor tab to determine your Love Factor result.

Love Factor

Property	Market	Address	Units	TM	Broker	Action	Count	Notes
Avery on 7th	Jax	123 Main St	150	Sean	Beau Beery with CBC	P	1	bad location
Harwood Oaks	Tally	456 Hello St	125	Jeffrey	John Smith with M&M	P	1	too old
Jasmine Court	Tally	789 Blanket Ave	219	Sean	Blair Jones with C&W	BO	1	discovered environmental issues
Lake Oaks	Orlando	4444 Blank St	335	Alice	Jill Michaels at JLL	P	1	price too high
Silver Creek	Gville	4444 Hello Rd	176	Sean	Blair Jones with C&W	UC	1	performing walk thrus on 8/15
Oakwood	Ocala	2211 MLK Dr	333	Alice	Arnold Akey with Colliers	C	1	closed 12/13/20 for $85k/unit

Deals Seen	6
Total Deals	20
Love Factor	30.00%

Action Key

P = Passed on Deal

UC = Under Contract

C = Closed

BO = Went to Contract, Backed Out

"TM" - Team Member

Two Tabs

| Love Factor | Market Closing Tracker | + |

Market Closing Tracker

Property Name	Address	Type	Sale Date	Year Built	Sold For ($)	Units	$/Unit	Avg. Rent ($)	Total SF	Sale/SF ($)	GRM
Promenade	600 Park Ave, Orange Park	Market	2/25/2020	1990	9,000,000	100	90,000	900	84,155	106.95	8.33
The Park at Placid	5200 US Highway 98 N, Lakeland	Market	3/12/2020	1993	24,000,000	220	109,091	900	169,546	141.55	10.10
The Deck Apts	6000 SW 75th Terr, Gainesville	Market	3/13/2020	2005	52,000,000	250	208,000	1,500	343,646	151.32	11.56
Victoria Apts	1700 Wells Rd, Orange Park	Market	3/17/2020	1986	35,000,000	300	116,667	1,000	227,234	154.03	9.72
Ocean View	1600 Dunlawton Ave, Port Orange	Market	3/18/2020	1988	40,000,000	320	125,000	1,100	238,784	167.52	9.47

Love Factor | Market Closing Tracker | +

Note: Only 5 closings were shown here for brevity, despite showing 20 for the "Total Deals" cell entry on the Love Factor spreadsheet.

YOU CAN'T BUY MORE DEALS UNLESS YOU SEE MORE DEALS.

My father-in-law likes to say, "Whatever you measure, improves." Knowing your Love Factor gives you concrete evidence as to whether you and your team are doing the right things to attract more opportunities to your business. It's simple: the more chances you get at buying, the greater the likelihood that you'll buy. Many factors affect your Love Factor, and they all come back to your brand and your reputation. Elite Investors understand this and work on their Love Factor every day.

What are these variables? And how can you be sure your team is maximizing them? You can't be on every phone call. You can't see every email they send. You can't watch their every move. And who is watching you? Who is making sure *you* aren't the problem affecting the brand, the reputation, and the number of deals you get to see? It's extremely difficult to have a perfect Love Factor, but striving to know about every opportunity in a timely manner is a worthwhile goal. So how do you know if your team is doing the right things? You ask every party outside of your company. What? Did I just say to ask everyone if you are the problem? Read on.

I'm a big fan of anonymous surveys that allow the respondent to give their honest opinion. Remember how I said this may make you uncomfortable? If you can get past this discomfort, you will unearth some powerful information that will grow your business. The people who know whether your team has a great reputation in the market are primarily brokers, but also outside attorneys, other investors, lenders, third-party property managers and asset managers, environmental consultants, site inspection companies, and anyone else you deal with in order to buy or sell a property.

The brokers are the ones most responsible for your Love Factor, but others who interact with you will tell colleagues how it was to deal with you, which could impact your Love Factor. For instance, if you hire a vendor and then argue the price with them, rush them unnecessarily, take your time paying them, and generally treat them poorly, they will *absolutely* tell their spouse, brokers, and other investors about you. Their bad experience will reach numerous people who will undoubtedly affect your Love Factor. So, let's talk about how you survey.

Elite Investors use surveys, and when asked, I point them toward Survey Monkey. I suggest the personal "Advantage Annual" plan, which at the time of this writing is just under $400/year, paid in advance. This plan allows unlimited surveys, unlimited questions, and up to 5,000 responses per month. The free plan that Survey Monkey offers allows one survey per month but only 40 responses. There should be more than 40 brokers or other investors and third parties in your market for this exercise. If you think there are fewer than 40 people who can affect your Love Factor, then you probably aren't specializing in a large-enough market. Your plan should be to survey, on an annual basis, every single relevant broker, referral source, and third-party person in every market in which you work. The survey should include reactions to every member of your team who interacts with the outside world.

The survey will be conducted through an email communication. Let every recipient know that by participating in the survey they will be entered in a drawing for something of value. Since it is anonymous, they can simply screen capture the survey completion screen and email that back as their entry in the giveaway. One Elite Investor is known to award the newest iPad. Others routinely give $500 in American Express gift cards. Give the respondent the choice of which person they had interaction with, so they can rate that person (or those people) specifically. The results will help you understand the strengths and weaknesses in your organization. Be sure to stress the anonymous nature of the survey so they can speak freely. I do not recommend sending the surveys one at a time so that you can game the system and discover the respondent's identity. It is dishonest at best, and it will likely ruin, rather than improve, your relationship. Let them know that the entire point of conducting this survey is to improve your relationship with them. Thank them for their honesty.

So, what questions do Elite Investors ask? Since the entire goal is to increase your Love Factor, all you really want to know is whether your team is contributing toward that goal; and if not, why not. You need these answers so you can take appropriate immediate action. Share the results of the survey with the team and develop a plan for improving on weaknesses and encouraging strengths.

Here are the four main questions that will give you powerful feedback on your brand. If you know what needs to be fixed in order to grow your business and you don't make the improvements, then you can't complain about your low Love Factor.

1. On a scale of 1-10, with 1 being "Not excited at all" to 10 being "Extremely excited," given the totality of your experience with this team member in 2020, how excited would you be to work with XYZ Holdings again if you had to work with this team member?

1 - Not excited at all	5 - Neutral	10 - Extremely excited

2. What could this team member improve to make your experience with XYZ Holdings even better? Select all that apply.

- ○ Communication skills
- ○ Attention to detail
- ○ Timeliness
- ○ Enthusiasm
- ○ Nothing
- ○ Other (please specify)

3. Which of the following did the team member do right that we can encourage him/her to continue to do? Select all that apply.

- ○ Communication skills
- ○ Attention to detail
- ○ Timeliness
- ○ Enthusiasm
- ○ Nothing
- ○ Other (please specify)

4. On a scale of 1-10, with 1 being "Not motivated at all" to 10 being "Extremely motivated," given the totality of your experience with XYZ Holdings as a company, how motivated are you to do more business with our firm?

1 - Not motivated at all	5 - Neutral	10 - Extremely motivated

Remember, all honest feedback is effective feedback. Whether they had a good experience or not, respondents will respect you for asking.

Another benefit to these surveys is accountability to yourself and your staff. When team members know at the end of the year this survey is going to be conducted, they will put in the work during the year. Your team members will have a general sense of the survey results just by sharing the monthly Love Factor with them. If the Love Factor is rising, or remains high, they must be doing something right. The brand is ascending thanks to their efforts—which is a reason to celebrate. One Elite Investor treats his staff every 6 months to a private dinner at his home with a chef from a popular local restaurant who prepares and serves the food.

I use surveys to gauge my performance as a real estate broker or for various market-related questions, and I've found that sending surveys early on Thursday morning works well. I then send a reminder email on Sunday when they are at home with potentially more time to fill out the survey. Remember, while the survey is extremely important to you, it is not as important to them. Be sure to keep the survey short and tell them this twice in the conveying email. I like to point out the time it would take to complete the survey (2 minutes). Following is a sample of the email you may send out to ask people to participate in the survey.

Dear Bob (use mail merge function of CRM to address them by their first name to make it more personal):

Every year we conduct a survey to determine how well we are doing in our goal to optimize your experience with us. Even if we didn't complete a deal together but we had communication in some way, no matter how minor or seemingly insignificant, we'd like to hear from you.

- Maybe you brought us a deal and we passed. We want to hear from you on this interaction.
- If we completed a deal, we want to know how we did.
- If you helped on a deal, whether it closed or not, we want to hear from you.
- Maybe you called a team member to learn about us. How did that interaction go?
- Maybe you sent us a deal and nobody responded. We definitely want to know about that.

We believe that if you have an outstanding experience with us every time, we'll be able to transact with you more frequently in the future. Your input is extremely valuable, so we will enter you in a drawing for a (name in detail the gift and value of the gift) as a thank you for the estimated 2 minutes of your time to complete the survey. (To be entered in the drawing, simply email a screen shot of the survey-completion screen.) Your answers are anonymous, so please answer with complete honesty. Below, please click on the name of the person you've dealt with this year and answer the ___ questions associated with them. If you've dealt with more than one person, we would really appreciate a response for each. Each survey completed increases your odds of winning the drawing.

Survey for Bob Smith: CLICK HERE
Survey for Sarah Black: CLICK HERE
Survey for Beth Henley: CLICK HERE

Survey for John Barry:	CLICK HERE
Survey for Frank Smith:	CLICK HERE

Thank you so much for your time. We really appreciate your investment in making our relationship more effective.

P.S. If you prefer to discuss a team member directly, just reply to me directly at Frank@xyzholdings.com for a time to talk, or call me at 123-456-7890.

Sincerely,

Frank Smith

CEO, XYZ Holdings

At this point, you may feel that a survey is unorthodox or just too much work. Keep in mind that Elite Investors do the things that an average investor doesn't (or won't). Asking dozens of people what they think about you is Elite level. Most of us think we are decent people who make the right decisions, are honest, have integrity, and are like-able, but what we think of ourselves is not our brand. If you have a low Love Factor, you are probably deceiving yourself about your reputation in the market. You're being passed over by Elite Investors, over and over again, for some reason. There are many excuses, but the reality is that every Elite Investor has risen above the average performance in the market. The actions of Elite Investors can be learned. If you aspire to reach that level, there are no excuses for not at least attempting to increase your Love Factor.

An Elite Investor...	An Average Investor...
Ensures that partners and staff are causing more opportunities to appear.	Has no idea which staff members are holding them back from more opportunities.
Meticulously tracks their "Love Factor" throughout the year to ensure the most opportunities.	Doesn't have a Love Factor concept in use.
Rewards productive staff members, helps those who aren't, and gets rid of those who inhibit growth.	Holds on far too long to those who inhibit growth.
Is not afraid to ask what they can improve to gain more business together.	Is afraid to hear criticism about themselves and their organization.

Action Steps:

- Maintain a Love Factor spreadsheet that lists every property presented to the team by a broker or investor. Honesty of inputs by your staff is key. The Love Factor equation is total number of deals that were brought to you, divided by total number of deals that closed in the market. This is shown as a percentage.

- It is paramount to track every closing in the markets you work in. This spreadsheet can simply be called the Market Closing Tracker and can be a second tab on the Love Factor spreadsheet. Obtain this Market Closing Tracker information from a broker, rather than internally, because otherwise it would be a tremendous time commitment on the part of your staff.

- Set up a Survey Monkey account. Get the Personal "Advantage Annual" plan, which at the time of this writing is just under $400/ year paid in advance. The plan allows unlimited surveys, unlimited questions, and up to 5,000 responses per month.

- Set your CRM to notify you every year to conduct performance surveys on all transaction team members by surveying the brokers (and investors and other trades) in your market.

- Tell the recipients that their answers are anonymous so they can answer truthfully about your team members. Enter respondents in a drawing for a reward for participating. (To be entered in the drawing, they should simply email a screen shot of the survey-completion screen.) Make that reward a worthwhile one.

- Send the survey on a Thursday, and then again on Sunday. After you get the results, meet with your team members individually to discuss the conclusions and how to get better.

- The survey will have a link for each person on your team so that the respondent can do the survey for the person(s) they dealt with during the year.

- The Love Factor spreadsheet will be reviewed monthly, quarterly, and annually.

- After each review of the survey results and the corresponding Love Factor spreadsheet, you will be able to identify strengths and weaknesses of your transaction team members and take appropriate action. Be sure to celebrate improvement.

- You may also consider researching, through Google and other means, the Net Promotor Score (NPS) methodology for evaluating your team's performance from one period to the next. Roughly two thirds of Fortune 1000 companies use the methodology, which measures the loyalty between provider and customer.

Now that we've worked through how Elite Investors obtain feedback about how the world sees their brand, we're ready to talk about a critical factor that helps Elite Investors build their brand... *response time*. Elite Investors have had powerful results with these objectives, which are described in detail in the next chapter.

CHAPTER 4

RESPOND QUICKLY

No one ever said, "I love doing business with XYZ.
They take only a week or two to respond."

We have a saying in my office: "Time kills deals." Every Elite Investor I've worked with always moved lightning fast. It's a compulsion to them: they *do not* want to lose a deal. They would be mortified if they lost a deal because they took too long to respond. Good brokers have an unquenchable need for speed—it's how they get paid—and Elite Investors empathize with the brokers in this regard.

When a broker secures a listing on a productive apartment complex, the broker doesn't wonder whether they'll sell it. They *know* they'll sell it. The task is choosing *which* buyer is best for their seller. There will always be many more investors for every decent listing. This means that a buyer has to compete for every new listing… *even* off-market listings. The broker and the seller choose the winner.

Elite Investors, when selling, place high value on the probability of closing, not just the price and terms. So if there are always dozens, hundreds, or even thousands of buyers for any one listing, then how do a broker and seller choose the buyer? Beyond merely price and terms, numerous other buyer qualifications come into play. Price and terms are meaningless if you never close. Going under contract to a buyer who doesn't close wastes everyone's time and money and potentially sours other potential investors on the property.

So how does this tie to responding quickly? This is where Elite Investors think differently. Elite Investors know that in a perfect world, brokers want to bring their sellers the best offers from investors who consistently go the distance to closing without delay and drama. That's what makes sellers happy. So, who is more likely to be included in a broker's distribution list of buyers for a new listing? Would it be the buyer who never responds to new listings, never returns calls, never returns emails, takes forever to make an offer, takes too long in due diligence, takes too long to close, takes forever to reply to counters, and just generally takes their sweet time to respond to any correspondence whatsoever, if at all?

Or, is the broker sending new listings to Elite Investors who always answer the phone, return calls immediately, always respond to email, comment on every new listing sent, always submit offers extremely quickly on deals they like, always act fast during due diligence, and always show up to closing on time and without delays? I think you get my point.

ONE OF THE PRIMARY REASONS MOST AVERAGE INVESTORS DON'T TRADE ANYWHERE NEAR THE SAME CLIP AS ELITE INVESTORS IS BECAUSE THEY NEVER MADE IT ONTO THE BROKER'S LIST.

If there are an endless number of buyers for an asset, why would a broker or seller include those who show a pattern of slow response or even indifference? Who wants to keep sending deals to someone who never provides any feedback or returns any calls or emails? Nobody.

Investors get tons of emails and calls every day. Investors get new listings sent to them from markets they don't even buy in, they get "Just Closed" emails, market report emails, mailings, and the list goes on. Everyone is busy. Business moves at the speed of light. Use this to your advantage.

If the majority of investors are "too busy" to respond, it will set you apart immediately if you always respond. Providing feedback quickly goes a very long way with brokers. If your business is dependent on buying multifamily assets, and brokers sell the overwhelming majority of multifamily assets, Elite Investors know there is no better time spent than communicating frequently, consistently, and immediately.

Elite Investors do a great job of describing exactly what they want to buy. They continually provide feedback on every deal they receive, even those that don't interest them. Elite Investors are cordial with every email, every call, and every interaction. They pick up the phone and have a dialogue with each broker. For example, if you buy only 150+ unit deals, but you'd buy one that's 110 units under the right circumstances (because it was near another property you own), it's better to say that under conditions you'd buy 100+ units. You'd hate to miss out on a deal based on a technicality.

Take advantage of broker websites that send you assets based on a criteria page you can fill in. When you get listings that don't match your criteria, or market, or whatever, it's a mistake to *not* respond. It is the worst thing you can do! Brokers will eventually stop sending you anything. Instead, respond why it doesn't work and thank them for including you. Brokers are given a finite amount of time to sell an asset; the longer you take to respond, the more they tend to ignore you.

LET'S TAKE A MINUTE TO TALK ABOUT OFF-MARKET DEALS.

There are two types of off-market deals. The first is when a property is not on the market but a broker brings a single buyer to the owner of the property and delivers an offer that makes enough sense to the seller to proceed to a contract and subsequent sale.

The second type is when an investor deliberately hires a broker in an exclusive capacity to sell their property but doesn't want it publicly marketed.

Responding quickly is never more important than in off-market situations. When a broker brings a single buyer to a seller (the first type of off-market deal), do you think a broker would ever choose a buyer who has a history of slow or no response to deals presented? Of course not. This rare type of deal making is reserved for situations in which the broker has such confidence in the buyer (usually an Elite Investor) that they are willing to spend time offering on an asset that isn't for sale. They know their buyer will respond immediately and with strong offer terms.

For off-market deals where the seller deliberately hires a broker in an exclusive-listing capacity to sell the property quietly, Elite Investors know that brokers will narrow their offering to only the best buyers. Many brokers rank their list of investors in the same A-B-C fashion that investors use for brokers because they have to know where to invest their time most effectively. Brokers can't spend time trying to develop a relationship with a group that isn't responsive to new listings. Elite Investors are absolutely the first to get the call in any off-market scenario.

AN HOUR TODAY MIGHT MEAN MILLIONS OF DOLLARS OF PROFIT SOMEWHERE DOWN THE ROAD.

Elite Investors always respond to all brokers and investors wanting to do business with them. Even when the listing isn't even close to what they are looking for, Elite Investors still spend a few minutes getting to know the agent. They explain what they are looking for because it could set the stage for an agent to bring them one great deal during their lifetime. It might take ten years for this approach to pay off, but Elite Investors take that chance.

As I've worked with Elite Investors, I've crafted the following list to give you a sense of effective response times. Remember, consistency is key. The more responsive you are on every level of deal making, the more deals you'll see. A response can be as simple as an acknowledgement of receipt. Each deal is different and occasionally causes longer response times. The times below are accurate for the majority of deals. The sooner you can perform any of these tasks, while maintaining quality in your decision making, the more your positive reputation grows in the industry. The better your reputation, the more deals you'll see.

Action or Aspect	Respond within
You received an introductory call or email from a new broker in your market	48 hours
You received a "Just checking in" call or email from a broker (nothing urgent)	48 hours
You were offered a new listing (whether or not you have interest)	Within 18 hours
Discussed new listing; you like it and were asked to sign a Confidentiality Agreement (CA)	Within 8 hours
You received all deal material; time to submit a Letter of Intent (LOI)	Within 5 calendar days
Seller has received LOI and countered; now you need to counter or accept	Within 1 business day
Signed LOI is in place; you are to tour while contract is being constructed	Within 4 business days
You've toured and need to either adjust or accept offer	Immediately
All contract negotiations	Within 1 business day
Due-diligence periods (non-portfolio)	Up to 30 calendar days
Due-diligence periods (portfolio)	Up to 45 calendar days (up to 60 if multi-state)
Days to close after due-diligence period	Up to 45 calendar days

An Elite Investor...	An Average Investor...
Understands the competitive nature of multifamily investment.	Underestimates the number of investors with whom they compete.
Responds lightning quick at every stage of communication and transacting.	Responds when available to issues and questions.
Sees new listings first because brokers know they are quick to react.	Never makes it to the "first look" list of investors due to historically slow response time.
Spends time educating brokers on what they buy and quickly provides feedback on new listings.	Usually doesn't share criteria, or poorly communicates it to brokers. They rarely provide feedback on new listings.
Is the first to be called with new off-market listings.	Never hears about new off-market listings.

Action Steps:

Here are some actions that can help you respond more quickly. Quick action isn't reserved for brokers and investors alone. Remember, reputation is everything, and if you're slow to respond with any participant in a transaction, the word will spread that you are sloth-like and therefore to be avoided!

- Discuss your acquisition criteria with as many investment sales brokers as possible. Convey criteria that are broad enough that you see every possible asset that fits your profile. Conveying this information correctly will reduce the unnecessary calls and increase the number of opportunities you will see.
- Ensure that every member of your transaction team has the cell phone number of every broker saved in their phones so they know who's calling and can respond immediately. Reply to all broker calls, preferably by phone (email as a backup), within 48 hours.
- Have your IT administrator make certain every broker email address you have is "white listed" internally so that none of their emails go to spam. (You can do this yourself if you use Outlook. Right click on an email, select "Junk" in the drop-down menu, and then select "Never Block Sender"). You don't want to miss out on an incredible deal because new listings have been going to spam. Let the broker know, within 18 hours, that you received their email.
- If you have staff who receive snail mail on behalf of transaction team members, instruct those staff to make sure transaction team members see that mail promptly. Respond to mail received within 48–72 hours by email, text, or phone call. You could even take a picture of the mail piece and send it to them in email or text format to show you got it.

- Adhere to the response timetable above, and do your best to meet or beat the deadlines.

Now that we've established the importance Elite Investors place on response times in various aspects of communication and transactional dialogue, in the next chapter we'll cover how Elite Investors incentivize brokers to shower them with more opportunities than anyone else.

CHAPTER 5

COMPENSATE YOUR BROKERS

It isn't just about the money.

Elite Investors recognize the broker's commission is a tiny fraction of the amount of the deal. Elite Investors focus on the reward, so they are happy to pay a broker to sell their property or find them one to buy. This is how they ensure the job gets done to the best of the broker's ability *and ensure the broker is extremely motivated to do it for them over and over again.* This is the difference between Elite Investors and everyone else.

The monetary component of compensation is only a portion of the package. Compensation comes in other forms. Apply Maslow's Hierarchy of Needs to this situation. (See chart on next page.) When dealing with brokers, Elite Investors put themselves in the broker's shoes as much as possible. They understand the broker has the same needs they do. Elite Investors instinctively focus on the most crucial human needs from Maslow's chart.

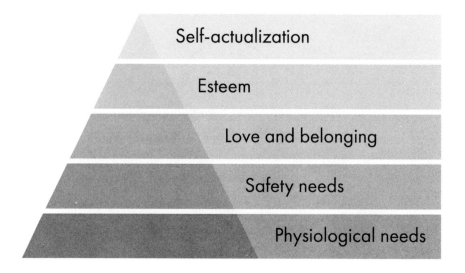

Physiological Needs: This is the basis of all human needs. Brokers and investors want to fundamentally provide basic food, water, and shelter for themselves and their families.

Safety Needs: Brokers and investors want to be able to earn steady money to provide security for their families and keep them healthy.

Elite Investors know Physiological and Safety needs are typically not issues for well-performing brokers. They focus instead on the following three Maslow principles to establish a tremendous working relationship that rewards both of them handsomely over a long career.

Love and Belonging: Elite Investors have figured out that developing friendships (a sense of connection) with their customers, co-investors, and brokers is very rewarding on several levels. For some brokers, this is more important than a commission. When a friendship is born from a professional relationship, it gives that broker (and investor) an added sense of accomplishment when he or she successfully completes a deal.

Elite Investors like forming bonds with others because it satisfies their need to connect. It's an added benefit when friends are able to do business together. I'm not saying you need to be every broker's best friend. It may never become the kind of relationship you have with your high school or college friends, but it is a friendship that a broker really cherishes. Elite Investors don't try to create fake friendships. They work hard to bond with as many people as possible, including brokers. Brokers are inspired by friendships with their customers.

Esteem: Esteem is composed of respect, self-esteem, status, recognition, strength, and freedom. The *Love and Belonging* portion of Maslow's Hierarchy is meaningful to brokers because the friendship is born of mutual respect for each other's craft in the multifamily business. This respect turns into friendship and a sense of connection; a bond that builds self-esteem in the broker (and the investor). It gives them more confidence in their craft. They get better at their craft, which leads to recognition and rewards. Recognition and reward can also come from the customer. Everyone wants to feel needed, respected, and recognized—to feel "esteemed." This is huge compensation for most brokers.

Self-actualization: This is the top of Maslow's Hierarchy. It's what we're all after, which is to feel like what we're doing personally and professionally is exactly what we're supposed to be doing in this life. It means reaching your potential—to become everything you're capable of becoming. As a result of being satisfied (having enough water, food, shelter, safety, friendships with customers, love, respect, and recognition), brokers feel like they are doing exactly what they are supposed to be doing. Having a sense of fulfillment only multiplies the desire to be better at what they do. When a broker reaches self-actualization, they are internally and consistently motivated to produce for investors during the rest of their careers.

Elite Investors understand that while a broker's commission is a small proportion of any deal, it is a huge component of a broker's motivation. Elite Investors never ask what's the least they can pay a broker to perform a transaction. They are constantly thinking about differentiating themselves from the herd. Let's look more closely at what brokers do and how they think. Our goal is to understand how fairness relates to motivation.

Multifamily brokerage is typically conducted by some of the best-performing commercial real estate brokers in the country. These transactions often have larger volume, involve more sophisticated clientele, have complex deal structures, have more sophisticated financing, and require the financial analysis of an extremely knowledgeable person. There are far fewer high-performing multifamily brokers than of any other asset category. And among those multifamily brokers, the 80/20 rule is usually in effect, meaning that about 20% of those brokers are doing 80% of the sales.

Multifamily brokers can be part of a publicly traded firm, a large national non-publicly traded firm, a franchise, or an independent (private company). Being part of a large firm does not guarantee performance. There are numerous examples of brokers at independent firms, or at the smaller franchise firms, who outperform large-firm brokers. The key issue is that the broker's net commission (the amount that they receive net to themselves) varies by type of firm. There are widely disparate internal commission split structures. Having knowledge of how different brokers are paid will help you understand the importance of fairly compensating the brokers you work with, in commissions and also in recognition, respect, and relationship.

Let's take a look at a simple example that will give you a sense of the way a $100,000 commission paid at closing to the brokerage agency is typically processed by that agency—and how much money reaches the pocket of the individual broker.

Here's the example:

	Structure Element	Calculation
A	Amount of gross commission paid to an agency	$100,000
B	Franchise or corporate fee, ranges from 0–10%; let's use 5%	– 5%
C	Gross profit for franchise or corporation	= $95,000
D	Amount retained by the agency—the house split—ranges from 20% to 50%; let's use 40%	– 40%
E	Gross profit for brokerage team	= $57,000
F	Split between brokers of the same team who worked on the deal, ranges from 20% to 80%; let's use 50%	– 50%
G	Net commission to the broker you worked with	= $28,500

Here are the details:

A. Let's say that the commission agreement called for a brokerage fee of 4% to be paid on a $2,500,000 transaction. This means that the broker will receive a check at closing in the amount of $100,000, which will be made payable to the broker's agency.

B. Many agencies have an agreement with their franchisor or parent company that calls for a franchise fee to be paid "off the top" for every commission received.

C. In this case, we're using 5% of the $100,000 commission, which means $5,000 is "sent to corporate," leaving $95,000 left to split between the company, or agency, and the brokers involved in the transaction.

D. Every broker has an agreed structure of commission split with the company for which they work. These structures vary widely and often have a progressive scale, which enables a broker to keep a larger share of the commission as his or her annual production volume increases. In this case, we'll use 40% of the commission as the amount retained by the company.

E. This means that 60% of the agency's $95,000 commission, equating to $57,000, is paid to the brokers who conducted the deal.

F. Many brokers work in teams today. In this case, we are assuming that two brokers worked on the deal and agreed to split the net commission on a 50/50 basis.

G. After splitting the deal into two equal parts, each broker nets $28,500. Remember that this is paid to them as independent contractors, and that they now must treat this as gross income for tax purposes. And the broker still has all the regular expenses of a typical business, including salaries (to an assistant or other), health insurance, marketing, accounting, etc.

The point is that when an investor pays a $100,000 commission, only a fraction goes to the salesperson's bank account. Elite Investors understand how this works at different brokerages. They understand that good multifamily brokers work thousands of hours, trying to find property for them to buy. It's a grueling process full of so much rejection, day in and day out, it would be sad to watch if it were a movie.

Here's the way one Elite Investor put it: "Investors take advantage of years of blood, sweat, tears, rejection, successes, experience, knowledge, relationships, and market intelligence from a broker for a very small percentage of the deal size. The investor doesn't have to pay a nickel for all that unless the broker produces a deal for them and then pays that nickel only upon closing. In what other industry does that happen?"

Understanding how fees are processed can help educate an investor on whether they are compensating a broker fairly. Every fee is potentially negotiable. There are no collectively set commission percentages among brokerages. Brokers cannot coordinate with other brokers to set commissions in a market. This is an antitrust-law violation called *price fixing*, which has criminal and civil consequences.

Brokers can only tell you what they would independently charge to provide specific services. They are compelled to keep the price of their services competitive in the market. Because of this competition, commissions within a specific market generally tend to be similar from one broker to the next. Over time you'll get an idea of the range of commissions that firms charge for a service when you deal with each of them.

If you ask a broker what they would charge for their service, the broker should respond with something like, "Mr. Investor, my firm would charge 3.0% to sell your 100-unit, $10,000,000 apartment complex in Daytona Beach, Florida." The broker should not respond with something like, "Mr. Investor, the standard set commission my brokerage and other brokers are charging is 3.0% to sell a 100-unit, $10,000,000 apartment complex in Daytona Beach, Florida." Be careful in how you ask about commissions; do not accidentally lead the broker toward a violation. If you do, you will be just as entangled in the consequences as the broker. A proper way to ask would be this:

"Mr. Broker, what commission would your firm charge me to sell my XYZ Apartments?"

Elite Investors always try to determine what is fair within a given market by asking agents what they charge. For example, let's say an investor spoke to ten brokers in their market and asked them individually what they'd charge to sell a specific asset and found the commission to range from 2.00% to 3.50%, with an average falling around 2.75%. If the investor then chose the broker they felt was most qualified, who quoted a 3.25% fee, would they negotiate to lower the fee? Not likely. How important is that half a percent? Is it worth demotivating that broker from bringing them more deals to buy in the future? Because that would likely be the result.

Elite Investors would argue that:

- If a half to one point on a sale is important enough to not do the deal, then they should never be doing the deal in the first place; and
- It doesn't make economic sense to potentially lose millions of dollars of business from a broker (especially a highly productive one) just because of an effort to devalue their worth to save a relatively tiny amount of money.

Elite Investors know that any broker can choose to include thousands of buyers in their buyer distribution list. Savvy investors differentiate themselves from other investors by taking a "big picture" view of the commission and its impact on the broker.

While Elite Investors aren't trying to pay smaller commissions to a broker, they also aren't just throwing away money. Occasionally, Elite Investors will take a creative approach to lowering the commission but also motivating the broker. As an example, an Elite Investor once asked me to take a lower commission on a very thin deal while simultaneously offering me the opportunity to list an asset for sale at a much larger commission. I've also been in a situation where an Elite Investor pulled me in on a purchase they were already working on, in order to compensate me to make up for a recent deal involving them where I wasn't fairly compensated by the other party.

In my experience, the majority of multifamily brokers don't ask for higher fees than what is typical in a market. They just want to be fairly valued for their skill. Elite Investors pay fairly, so they don't motivate brokers to tell other brokers, investors, and participants in a transaction how poorly they were treated.

Remember, the cancer created by trying to save a few bucks can spread like wildfire from broker to broker or broker to other investors, and the disease goes on. Elite Investors focus on their future pipeline of opportunities. If the majority of those opportunities are coming from brokers, it makes no sense to choose to devalue the broker's sense of worth to save a few bucks on one deal while threatening the loss of many other deals in the future.

The same concept applies when Elite Investors have engaged a broker to buy an asset. Oftentimes Elite Investors will engage brokers to find them assets to buy that meet their criteria. Some Elite Investors prefer to pay their broker's commission rather than having the seller pay, so that their offer is as enticing as possible to the seller. Elite Investors always agree to reasonable fees on the buy side, to keep the brokers motivated to find additional assets for them. And a one-half to one percent variation in commission doesn't make any difference to them, compared to an opportunity to earn a sizable profit down the road.

Elite Investors also treat commissions differently during the course of a transaction. For some investors it has become commonplace to lean on the broker when monetary issues arise. For instance, let's say we have a $20,000,000 apartment sale that is two weeks from closing. It was suddenly discovered that new flood maps came out right before closing and a tiny portion of the property now requires flood insurance. The resulting impact on the value is $150,000. The commission agreement calls for a fee of $300,000.

One party suggests that the buyer, seller, and broker evenly split the difference so they can all move to closing. The buyer and seller are each going to cough up an unexpected $50,000 and the broker, who doesn't own the property, hasn't had the benefits of the cash flows, doesn't get the benefit of the sale proceeds, and who had nothing to do with the flood zone determination, is asked to cough up nearly 17% of their commission ($50,000/$300,000). This means that the seller is taking home 99.75% of their proceeds, the buyer is paying 100.25% of the value of the property, and the broker is walking away with 83% of the agreed fee for procuring a successful buyer. Elite Investors don't let this happen. Remember, they see the forest, not the trees.

Elite Investors know that if the extra $50,000 the broker is being asked to pay was truly a difference maker on a $20,000,000 deal, then they should never be buying or selling the asset in the first place. Elite Investors put themselves in the shoes of the broker. Is it fair for the broker to be far more greatly impacted by a surprise expense than either of the other two parties? If the broker were to contribute the same percentage of their commission as the seller (assuming the seller paid the whole $150,000), then the broker would contribute $2,250 toward the flood issue ($300,000 x .0075). This is the economic reality of evenly sharing in the issue. Yet some investors choose to see the trees and not the forest. They make the short-term-thinking mistake of squeezing the broker and threatening to cancel the sale altogether. Elite Investors don't take advantage of the broker. They want to preserve that relationship so the broker will remain extremely motivated to bring them more deals.

WHEN BROKERS SEE AN ELITE INVESTOR PROTECT THEM AND VALUE THEM, THEY ARE EVEN MORE COMMITTED TO MAKING ADDITIONAL DEALS WITH THOSE ELITE INVESTORS.

An Elite Investor...	An Average Investor...
Always compensates brokers fairly in the buying and selling of assets.	Negotiates as small a commission as possible to close a transaction.
Understands there is more to a broker's incentive then monetary compensation.	Focuses on monetary compensation, the very bottom of Maslow's Hierarchy of Needs.
Compensates brokers in a way that leads to Self-Actualization.	Doesn't consider building up others to help them reach their potential.
Understands the commission structure of various brokerages and the impact on the broker's net compensation.	Doesn't know the different brokerage structures and their effect on the agent's net compensation.
Has a strong appreciation for the time and effort brokers expend to produce investment opportunities.	Underestimates, and therefore undervalues, the broker's time and effort to procure investment opportunities.
Knows that brokers will provide more opportunities if they are consistently compensated fairly, both monetarily and personally.	Never considers the long-term effect on future opportunities from brokers as a result of unfair compensation.
Endeavors to protect, not cut, brokers' fees during a transaction when issues arise between a buyer and seller.	Is indifferent to the broker's outcome; all is fair in love and war.

Action Steps:

- Study Maslow's Hierarchy of Needs and buy related books; understand the psychology behind how humans are motivated. The famous book, *How to Win Friends and Influence People* by Dale Carnegie is a masterpiece in describing this concept and should be read often.

- Learn what commission ranges are in each market, for various price points, and for each job (buy or sell) by interviewing brokers *individually* on what they would charge in various situations. Be careful that you do not lead the broker into a violation of antitrust laws.

- Look back over a transaction that you completed in which the broker's fee was reduced just before closing. As you look at that situation in hindsight, would you change how the situation was handled?

In Chapter 5, we learned how Elite Investors keep brokers highly motivated to bring them more deals by making sure they feel fulfilled in their careers and fairly compensated. In the next chapter, we look at one of the most important skills Elite Investors possess that leaves investors, brokers, and other related parties to a transaction yearning to do more deals with them.

CHAPTER 6

PUT YOUR SELLER (OR BUYER) HAT ON

Change your perspective to see more clearly. Practicing
appropriate deal etiquette and empathy are massive
moneymakers for Elite Investors.

I've often asked myself, "If a seller is a buyer and a buyer is a seller, why is there still so frequently a disconnect in contract negotiations?" The answer is empathy. It's about not letting selfishness, ego, and short-term thinking cloud your judgment.

Elite Investors check their egos at the door, while average investors treat negotiating as a game they have to win. The second you turn a transaction into a game you have to win, you've lost more than you'll ever be able to calculate. Elite Investors know all parties to a transaction are watching how they handle every decision. When you express empathy in every interaction and every decision, everyone around you notices.

Empathy in deal making is so rarely exercised because the mantra of most deal makers is to win and squeeze every drop of return possible at all costs. These ordinary investors fail to appreciate the negative tsunami that then occurs. The tough-guy approach to negotiating rarely works long term. Sometimes you win a negotiation, but ultimately it will cost you deals you'll never see. This chapter describes the way Elite Investors operate in a transaction, from negotiating the offer to due diligence to closing.

Before Elite Investors even submit an offer, they spend time researching whomever they'll be dealing with. If they are the buyer, they want to know who the seller is as a person and who advises them. They try to find answers to questions like these:

- Where is the seller from?
- Where did they go to school, and what is their education?
- How old are they?
- Are they married? Have kids?
- What do their kids do for a living?
- What are some of the seller's accomplishments?
- What are their hobbies?

They also investigate:

- Social media profiles to look at pictures, at causes they care about, at things they comment on, and so forth.
- Articles about them or articles they've written.
- All the assets they own and locations, what they bought them for, and what they've sold others for.
- How long they've been in the business, where they get their equity, and how their ownership entity is structured.

- Their motivation for selling and what they intend to do with the money.

THE ENTIRE PURPOSE OF THIS RESEARCH IS TO HUMANIZE THE TRANSACTION.

If the Elite Investor is the seller, they want to know the same things about the buyer. Finding commonalities between the parties and understanding their motivations makes it far easier to negotiate a deal and handle issues as they arise during a transaction. *Every* deal has issues that arise. How much easier is it to reach compromise on terms or issues if you both went to the same school, or both have teenage girls, or both love cars, or both have the same investing philosophy, or both know several of the same people? Elite Investors strive to find common ground in order to make the deal run more smoothly and build a reputation that will allow them to transact more often and, hopefully, more than once with the same people.

During contract negotiations, Elite Investors pay close attention to how business is typically transacted in a given market. Let's say that the seller almost always pays for the title in that market. An Elite Seller wouldn't counter an offer by shifting that cost to the buyer. It would create immediate ill will with the buyer. If it is typical that the buyer is the one to order a new survey, then it doesn't make sense to turn in an offer that orders the seller to provide a new survey. Even these seemingly incidental costs can have huge effects on the other party and their willingness to make a deal with you.

Humans are easily offended. Many investors have big egos and can become angry quickly. Why ask for things that you know aren't typical of a market? If you don't know the customs in a market, find them out in advance by talking to your broker or other investors.

Elite Investors don't ask for things that are totally out of the ordinary because they know the other side's mood can completely change. The other side will likely become less willing to compromise, and they'll spread the word to others on how difficult you are as a negotiator.

Think about it: if you were selling your car and a buyer submitted an offer that included you paying for their tax, tag, title, and their gas for a year, how would that make you feel? You probably wouldn't even respond. If there are hundreds of data points to suggest how a typical transaction or fee is handled in a certain market, why go against that? Whether it's greed or ignorance, the result will be the same: perhaps you will win the battle, but you will surely lose the war.

When price becomes the last point of agreement in a transaction, I've seen Elite Investors reveal their underwriting and assumptions. You might think this is like turning over your social security information and the password to your Charles Schwab account, but let's think about it. If the deal is about to die and there are no other cards on the table, Elite Investors try everything they can to make a deal. They don't throw in the towel and just assume the seller or buyer is unreasonable. When Elite Investors are the seller, they show why their price makes sense and if they are the buyer, they show their work to figure out where the disconnect is. I've seen more than one deal rescued in this fashion.

I've seen sellers (and brokers), when they show their work, point out incorrect assumptions about flood insurance, renewal rates, one-time capital expenditures, recurring maintenance, or future property taxes, as well as just plain input errors. Technology is wonderful, but it is subject to human errors. Even the brightest minds in the business make mistakes; I've seen numerous parties in one company miss the same error on the same transaction. When you look at numbers all day every day, it's bound to happen. A fresh set of eyes is so important.

A seller can point out errors or incorrect assumptions to help increase the buyer's offer, and a buyer can point out items that a seller wasn't thinking of in order to justify the buyer's offer. But unless you "show your work," the deal just dies and goes away when it has the potential to be saved.

Elite Investors know there is no single correct way to underwrite a deal. Revealing your financial analysis is *not* like giving up your social security number. One's underwriting methods are unlikely to be some magically unique approach to evaluating assets. Not to oversimplify, but it really just comes down to assumptions about certain line items. Ideally, the parties view the assumptions, and therefore the achievable return, the same way. The final step is for the buyer to decide that the risk is worth the agreed return.

If an Elite Investor has shown their work and corrected all errors and there is still disconnect on price due to the risk and reward scenario, then all parties should be able to walk away satisfied they did everything they could. There is no harm in that scenario. By knowing where they stand on rate of return, the parties can later resurrect the deal quickly and execute at a mutually agreed price. Elite Investors never want to lose a deal over something that could have been prevented by being more transparent.

ELITE INVESTORS ALSO CHOOSE ATTORNEYS WHO SHARE THEIR BELIEFS ABOUT DEAL MAKING AND EMPATHY.

This is huge! Every Elite Investor I know is represented by an attorney with whom I thoroughly enjoy working. They show empathy in transactions, and they truly thrive on doing deals rather than suspiciously searching for ways the other party is trying to get the upper hand. Unfortunately, the opposite is often true. Some investors choose attorneys who thrive on redlining as many words as they can so their client thinks they are really good. When they find a clause they don't like, instead of thinking about solutions, they build up the issue to be more important than it is. I've seen attorneys redline the word "property" and change to "Property" throughout an entire document, adding over 200 redlines. The attorney could just point out to the other attorney that once there is agreement on the finer points, that they should replace the word throughout the entire document. Attorneys are used to seeing that kind of redlining, so it is no big deal to them. But when investors open a document like that, they are completely deflated, angry, and aggravated. Even if most of the redlines are grammatical, it still sours the review process.

Elite Attorneys have an encouraging tone that a deal can get done; they give realistic probabilities on issues, never raise their voice, and never start building up the other side as villains. These attorneys know that the more deals they can help their clients do, while still keeping them safe, the more those clients will use them and help them grow their own law practice. Also, Elite Attorneys know that they contribute to the Elite Investor's reputation as well. They don't want to be seen as difficult and unpleasant. They know their behavior will affect future deal flow.

Choose attorneys who have the right balance of deal making and keeping you safe. Choose ones that play nice with other attorneys, even when the other attorneys are difficult. If you don't have an attorney yet, ask around. In any given market, you'll start to hear the same recommended names come up, or ones to avoid, if you ask enough people. Then interview them, preferably in person, and see how your interests align.

Once Elite Investors are under contract, this is where Elite Attorneys really shine. Apartment deals take work to close. It's just the nature of the asset that is being transacted. Apartment complexes have lots of kitchens, bathrooms, clubhouses, pools, acreage, tenants, staff, and so on. It is impossible for a transaction to proceed completely seamlessly from contract to closing. There are just too many moving parts. Elite Investors know it isn't the issues that arise, it's how you deal with those issues and the people involved.

PUTTING ON THE HAT OF THE OTHER SIDE OF THE TRANSACTION WILL HELP YOU SEE MORE CLEARLY.

Every decision you make in a transaction has consequences as a positive or negative effect on your brand and your reputation. Elite Investors are constantly asking themselves, "Okay, if I decide such and such, how will all the people involved think of me?" or "Is it the right thing to do?" or "Is there a better way that is fairer to everyone?"

In my experience, the majority of issues that become the most fiercely contentious during a transaction are small monetary issues (as a percentage of the price), *not* big monetary issues. Many of these small issues were unknown to the buyer and seller before the contract was signed, but often become bigger sticking points than much larger issues when trying to move forward on a deal. I have had more problems keeping a deal alive when a $20,000 issue on a $10,000,000 property surfaces than a $500,000 issue on the same property.

When a $500,000 issue arises that neither party knew about, it is a large-enough expense that both sides know the other party cannot move forward unless it's worked out. They usually work it out because it's too big to avoid. In contrast, a $20,000 issue often gets one party super annoyed that the other party is making such a big noise about a small expense. Egos come in to play and, before you know it, there is absolute hatred on both sides. "Can you believe this idiot? He's coming to me with a $20,000 issue on a $10,000,000 transaction!" The other side is saying, "What's wrong with this person? It's just $20,000 on a $10,000,000 deal. All he/she has to do is handle it, and I'll close." It happens *all... the... time.* It's like watching two children fight over the most insignificant toy.

ELITE INVESTORS NEVER THREATEN THEIR REPUTATION BY MAKING A BIG STINK OVER SMALL ISSUES.

When Elite Investors are sellers, they are completely transparent about all features of the property. Even though commercial real estate is usually a *caveat emptor* ("buyer beware") business, Elite Investors know that by not revealing all pertinent information, those details could come back to haunt them. If the seller is transparent, the buyer won't automatically assume the seller is being intentionally deceptive and is thus untrustworthy in all aspects of the transaction.

Caveat emptor means the buyer alone is completely responsible for finding any issues or concerns on the property before buying it. The principle is that the seller can't be held liable for issues the buyer found after closing. The buyer must complete their inspections thoroughly and live by the results. Elite Investors know it isn't worth staying silent on known issues in hopes the buyer doesn't find them.

It's such a reputation killer because those who get "wronged" do everything they can to spread the word about those who supposedly wronged them. Beyond the reputation damage, it's a huge waste of time to deal with a potential lawsuit after the deal closes. Trying to pass your problems off to the next investor is a shortsighted way of doing business and will lead to a short investment career.

Once under contract, the Elite Investor (acting as a seller) goes out of their way to run the management and leasing of the property to the highest standards to demonstrate to the buyer they care about them and want them to have the best buying experience. I've seen Elite Investors replace air conditioners when needed rather than keeping them alive till closing, change-out dead flowers, replace pool pumps that died a week before closing, and pressure-clean buildings and sidewalks while under contract. They seek opportunities to impress the buyer because (a) it's what they would do if they continued to own, (b) as a percentage of the deal, these things are typically miniscule, and (c) the benefit to their reputation of going above and beyond in caring for the property *during* the contract period leaves a good, lasting impression on everyone involved.

Elite Investors will forward pictures of repairs they've made to items that the buyer would've never even known about, just to demonstrate good faith. Elite Investors conduct so much repeat business because they consistently make the deal as painless as the circumstances allow. They know this is how they would want to be treated if they were buying.

Elite Investors also shine during the due-diligence period as the buyer. An average buyer may say something like this: "We have our Phase 1 vendor coming by Monday at 1 p.m.; please make sure someone from the property is there to get them inside 10% of the units." The Elite Investor *asks*, "When would be the best time for our Phase 1 vendor to tour 10% of the units, and whom should they meet?"

The average investor will say, "We need to inspect all 150 units, and we'll need three of your staff members to accompany our three teams for two days on Tuesday, starting at 8 a.m." The Elite Investor *asks*, "We intend to inspect all 150 units, but we want to be as considerate of your staff's time and daily obligations as possible. Internally, we can disperse as many as three teams at one time so we can get out of your hair more quickly. What works best for your operations?" There is a big difference between telling and asking. When people feel like you're making an effort to work with them, it buys tremendous good will.

Elite Investors take a long-term view when making current business decisions. They focus on the profitability of the asset over a long holding period. Does a $75,000 unforeseen issue in a deal today have real significance when a $4,000,000 profit can be realized five years later? Elite Investors certainly don't give in on every issue; but if challenges arise that are nobody's fault, or even are in a grey area, does it make sense to threaten walking out on a deal? Elite Investors never let ego trump sound financial decision-making and long-term deal flow.

In summary, Elite Investors are always measuring the long-term risk/reward equation in all their interactions with the parties of a deal, both during and after the deal. Every decision has consequences. Elite Investors aren't angels. They are faced with the same tough decisions in deal making as everyone else, but their talent is having trained their brains to first think of others. They seek to do the right thing rather than winning an argument. Because this talent is so rare, Elite Investors become instantly noticeable. Some Elite Investors are naturally empathetic, but many have learned it.

EMPATHY IS THE MOST UNDERRATED ADVANTAGE ANY INVESTOR POSSESSES WHEN COMPETING AGAINST OTHERS FOR A VERY SMALL SUPPLY OF DEALS.

An Elite Investor...	An Average Investor...
Employs empathy to solve problems, close more deals, and protect their reputation.	Solves problems with their own wellbeing as the primary consideration.
Seeks a win-win solution in deals.	Uses a "take or leave it" approach to deal making.
Spends considerable time researching commonalities with the other party to personalize the transaction, form bonds, and do more deals together in the future.	Typically has no clue who the other party is and the company they represent.
Doesn't veer from market norms in their offers or the way business is conducted in that area.	Makes offers and conducts business based solely on "the way we always do it."
Doesn't hesitate to share their underwriting when buying, or explain their value calculation when selling.	Walks away from a deal rather than share their underwriting or assumptions.
Chooses attorneys who share their philosophy on empathy, transparency, rationality, and deal closing.	Chooses attorneys who are overwhelmingly one sided, irrational in contracts, and uncaring about the damage to their investor client's reputation.

An Elite Investor...	An Average Investor...
Never allows insignificant issues to derail a closing; instead, concentrates on the forest, not the trees.	Argues every single issue out of principle, regardless of significance; sees the trees, not the forest.
Goes out of the way to be transparent with all material facts affecting value.	Remains silent and hopes something isn't discovered.

Action Steps:

- Learn who the other side is: where they are from, their education, age, sex, marital status, age and occupation of kids, their company, experience, accomplishments, hobbies, social media profiles, past jobs or companies they've owned, articles about or by them, as well as other properties they own.

- Find out the motivation for selling (or buying) and what they intend to do next. If you are asked these questions, reveal your answer ahead of time and answer honestly.

- Don't ask for things in a transaction that may be unusual for the market. Play by the rules of the market or you'll start off deal-making on bad footing.

- If price valuation is the last point of disagreement, show your work. The worst that can happen is that you lose the deal anyway. Opening up your underwriting for the other side to see is a great way to try to find common ground and keep the deal alive.

- When drawing up the contract, determine which points are most important to you and why. Share your conclusions ahead of time with the other party.

- Make certain your attorney is a deal maker and not a deal breaker. Deal-making attorneys check their ego at the door by focusing less on showing their client how smart they are and more on getting to "yes" while keeping their client safe.

- When disagreements on contractual issues arise, put yourself in the other side's shoes. Consider everything you know about them and make decisions based on that information, while not ignoring your own priorities. Elite investors are masters of empathy. Train your brain to exercise empathy on a regular basis. Once you master empathy, your deal-making world will blossom.

- Reveal to a buyer all relevant information affecting value in a transaction. The result of not doing so can be devastating.

- During the due-diligence period, continue to operate your property at maximum potential to show the buyer that you have their best interest at heart.

- During the due-diligence period, go out of your way to reveal all repairs/replacements, even if the buyer would never have known about it. Elite Investors know it builds trust and reputation to point out any pertinent issue. As a buyer, an Elite Investor plans in advance with the seller exactly what inspections they want and asks for guidance from the seller on the best way to achieve those with minimal disruption to tenants and staff. Elite Investors go out of their way to show sellers how much they respect their asset.

In this chapter we discussed the incredible power of displaying empathy in deal making and the return on investment as a result. The following chapter describes how Elite Investors become a magnet for every listed deal in a market.

CHAPTER 7

SHARE THE LOVE

Don't tie yourself to one agent. Wait a minute!
I'm a broker. Why would I say that?

The markets I cover have approximately 60 full-time multifamily specialists. There are dozens of part-time and residential real estate agents who also dabble in multifamily sales. Even though I try to provide every imaginable service to the Elite Investors that I track, does it make sense from their perspective to commit solely to me for buying and selling multifamily properties? *This may surprise you, but no.*

Elite Investors do their best to be as approachable as possible to all brokers because it greatly improves the number of deals they see, and thus the number of deals they could potentially close on. They encourage calls from almost all brokers and spend time educating them on their criteria and expectations for a successful relationship. Like throwing a casting net, the wider the cast, the better your chances of catching fish. The same goes for brokers: the more of them you befriend, the more deals you see.

While it's true a disproportionate share of the sales in any one market is done by a minority of the brokers (80/20 rule), it's still wise to court them all. Think about it mathematically. Let's say there are 50 closings of conventional assets of 100 units or more per year. Let's also say there are 60 brokers in that market who are either full or part time in multifamily sales. We'll assume 40 of those 50 closings (80%) were done by the top 12 of the 60 brokers (20%). Is it still worth communicating with the other 48 brokers over the course of a 10-year period? If you did, wouldn't you have a better chance at winning at least one of the other 100 closings in that 10-year period (50 – 40 = 10 closings x 10 years) controlled by the 80%? If you accomplished just one of those 100 closings and you made a multimillion-dollar profit, was it worth it? Elite Investors emphatically say "yes," but they strive to earn many more than just one of those other 100 closings.

Elite Investors may have favorite brokers, but they don't *publicly* advertise this. They know that if they showed favor to only a couple of brokers for listings and purchases, then the dozens of other brokers would feel like there wasn't much of a chance to earn their business. As a result, brokers would bring them fewer deals.

Using your favorite brokers is normal; just don't announce to all the other brokers that you only use a certain broker. Some investors choose only one broker to work with because they are old friends or college roommates, or they just generally work well together. The challenge for those investors is that the broker is getting the majority of professional benefit from that relationship. There are dozens of other brokers in the market who are purposely not showing the deals they list to those "committed to just one broker" investors. Those investors are potentially missing tens of millions of dollars in deals that they never get to see, or at least never get to see until dozens of other investors have already turned the asset down.

Elite Investors are particularly diplomatic in "sharing the love" when it comes to reselling assets that were brought to them by a broker. Elite Investors are aware there is a strong hope by brokers that if they bring an investor a successful deal, the investor will list the property with them in the future when it is time to sell. Brokers know this is not a guaranteed arrangement, but it's something they hope to earn. Elite Investors always try to reward a hard-working broker with the resale instead of playing favorites. If an Elite Investor chooses not to list with the broker who brought them the deal, they explain clearly to the broker why they made their choice, in a diplomatic manner that leaves the door open to future deals together. Elite Investors never want to burn bridges.

Elite Investors aim for the best Love Factor result they can possibly achieve. By cultivating as many broker relationships as possible, they see a higher percentage of new deals than anyone else. While it is the seller who makes the ultimate decision on which buyer to choose in a competitive bid scenario, the broker typically controls which buyers see the opportunity. Make no mistake, many multifamily assets are shown to a broker's best buyers before the opportunity ever becomes public.

Whether the asset is mass marketed or presented in an off-market capacity, Elite Investors want to make sure they are at the top of the list for new listings. They know that brokers want to do business with investors who respond quickly, inspect quickly, close on time without drama, and are open to additional transactions with them. Sharing the love is one of many reasons why Elite Investors are often promoted above other potential bidders by listing brokers.

The ultimate goal of Elite Investors is to have every broker in the markets they follow wanting to bring them deals. They motivate the brokers by giving them a fair shot at doing more business with them. The best way to tell if you are sharing enough love is to look at your

Love Factor spreadsheet. If you're seeing a lower percentage of the deals that close in the markets you work in, then you aren't working with as many brokers as you should in those marketplaces. Keep your mind open to doing deals with any broker who is productive, knowledgeable, and likable.

An Elite Investor...	An Average Investor...
Reaches out to build rapport with all brokers in a market who could bring them future deals.	Reaches out to a fraction of the brokers in the market and builds very little rapport.
Doesn't *publicly* announce broker favoritism.	Actively publicizes their preferred broker(s) and never considers others.

Action Step:

- As you begin meeting with brokers in person, via Zoom, and talking on the phone, let it be known that you are open for business. Tell them for any deal they bring, you would expect to sell with them in the future. Tell them you are happy to pay a commission on an acquisition if the seller will not. This will go a long way. Tell every broker they have an equal shot to transact with you in the future.

In the first seven chapters of the book, we have discussed in depth all the things Elite Investors do to significantly outperform the average investor in transacting. In the bonus chapter we'll reveal an often-overlooked secret weapon Elite Investors keep top of mind that boosts their reputation in the marketplace, which in turn nets them more deals and better relationships with their partners and attracts more investors and higher quality staff.

BONUS

FAMILY AND FRIENDS COME FIRST

Having a work/life balance attracts the highest quality staff, partners, investors, and brokers.

Real estate investing is an extremely demanding occupation. In the early stages of real estate investing, you are so hungry for information, for success, for your next deal that you never notice the hours you're putting in. You get your first deal done, and then your second, and then your fifth. Before you know it, you're so busy you begin to feel like you could work 24/7 and never catch up. And the better you get at investing, the busier you become. It's an exciting yet vicious cycle if you don't control it. Whether you're a smaller investor who does deals as a side hustle to build wealth for retirement, or you're a medium-size investor making a living doing this, or you've built a large regional or national investment company, you must have the right work/life balance or you're going to hit a wall. As we all know, the "crash and burn" often has to occur just to get our attention.

NOT ALL ELITE INVESTORS HAVE A GOOD WORK LIFE BALANCE, BUT ELITE INVESTORS CAN GET MORE BALANCE BECAUSE THEY DON'T HAVE TO HUSTLE SO HARD TO FIND OPPORTUNITIES.

Many investors have echoed the same "hitting a wall" stories to me. Most are males between 40 and 55 years old who are at the top of their game, and who seem like they have a great life. They have a spouse, kids, dog, nice house, and expensive cars, and they live in a great neighborhood. Here's a story about Joe, a friend, with a typical story.

Joe had been buying small multifamily properties since the late 1990s. As a 22-year-old with no spouse and no kids, he would work his tail off. He yearned for the grind. He loved it. He would grind for 80+ hours for weeks at a time. He did this for years. He eventually got married, had kids, and was growing his personal brand as an Elite Investor. He'd wake up every day at 4:30 a.m., work out, eat breakfast, work till 7:00 p.m., eat dinner, then work until midnight every day, 7 days a week. But the work started to grind him down. Nonetheless, as a Type-A personality, he kept working insane hours, doing more and more business. He spent as much time as he could with his wife and kids, but never as much as he wanted. If you asked his kids what their dad liked to do, they would always say, "He works."

By 2017, after being in the investment business for 18 years, Joe told me he was beginning to have a hard time breathing. He said it started off slow and for months just felt like he couldn't get a full breath. He wasn't concerned, yet, but the symptom never went away. He said he only got relief when he finally fell asleep. He was so busy and had so many deals he was working, he felt like he couldn't just stop or even slow down. Whenever we talked, he genuinely believed he'd be able to catch up on his work, but it never happened. Every day, more work piled up.

By 2018, the "elephant" on his chest was getting heavier. Now, he was worried because his breathing range kept getting smaller each day. He felt like he was suffocating. In February of that year, he called me and said that he had his first panic attack. He seriously thought he was going to die right there at the gym because he thought he was having a heart attack, not a panic attack. He was rushed to the hospital and underwent all sorts of tests. The tests indicated that he was healthy. The doctor said he was just stressed out. He argued that point with the doctor. He said he had nothing to be stressed about. He'd always been in real estate, always done deals, always had a big workload, and that his life was great.

When Joe got home from the hospital, he got back to work to catch up on the 5 hours he missed in the emergency room. A month later he had another panic attack. Back to the emergency room, more tests—still perfectly healthy. This time, though, Joe finally conceded to the doctors that he was suffering from too much stress.

With help from his wife and friends, Joe decided to completely change his ways. He met with a counselor to figure out why he needed to work so much to achieve some undefined level of success, even when he didn't need any more money or security. He discovered he was just never content. He always felt like he had to do more, achieve more, be the best. It was part ego, for sure. Over the years he had let his career be what defined him. He lost focus on what was actually important. He was spending so much time trying to be something he thought was important, when no one really cared about how many assets he bought or how much money he had.

Now, Joe has his work week down to 50 hours per week. He never works past 6:00 p.m. Monday through Friday, and he never works on the weekends unless it is something he actually enjoys. Now he is building awesome memories with his family, he has truly learned what contentment is, and his business has never been better! Removing that elephant from his chest has made him a better person. He is a better employer with his associates, he has more deals brought to him, and he just smiles more now.

Please allow me to relate, personally for a moment, to Joe's story. I've always held lunches several times a week with customers and all the related people in my industry (property managers, lenders, appraisers, attorneys, inspectors, etc.). When I'm at those lunches, I often hear stories from my companion about how they built a name, became really successful, got really stressed, and endured health issues. Some of the folks recovered and changed their lives; some had to fight off suicidal thoughts and depression. I try to tell Joe's story when I can (partly to remind myself), in hopes of helping to broaden someone else's perspective.

John Pencavel of Stanford University studied productivity. In his research, he found that as you increase the number of hours, productivity increases, but only up to a point. After 50 hours a week, the growth in productivity slows down. Past 55 hours, productivity plummets.

Real estate investing is a magnet for Type-A personalities, high achievers with extreme work ethics. They yearn for financial success and will work themselves to exhaustion to achieve it. They want the house, the cars, the toys, and an endless number of units. Please take a moment to consider how content you really are. Broaden your perspective. Joe is proof that once you learn to be content in your life, and you make family and friends your top priority, your business can be healthier than it's ever been. Committing to your hobbies, family, and friends from a time perspective forces you to make better, more efficient decisions in your business because you are controlling the total time you allocate to work.

When you make family and friends a priority and you get your business back on a more reasonable time commitment, you will become a different person. You will attract higher quality staff to your company, and your existing staff will follow your lead in living a healthier lifestyle. More investors will want to invest with you. Who wants to invest with a stressed-out partner who may not live through the asset's holding period? Best of all, you'll have more time to simply think about your business, instead of constantly trying to keep up, and you'll come up with even more ideas about how to accelerate your status as an Elite Investor.

An Elite Investor...	An Average Investor...
Places the highest importance on maintaining a balance of family, friends, and personally gratifying endeavors.	Places the highest importance on business growth. Family, friends, and hobbies come second.
Places hard limits on the daily work schedule to allow for healthy non-work-related activity.	Works with no limits or consideration to non-work-related activity.
Has learned how contentment, not complacency, makes them better investors, bosses, spouses, and parents, and more attractive clients to brokers.	Thinks contentment is a weakness that slows their growth, making them unattractive clients to brokers.

CONCLUSION

By this point, you've absorbed many ideas about how the most dominant investors perform. You've seen that they use a variety of techniques, plus the application of unique mindsets and personal commitments to be not only powerful, not only effective, but dominant. If you want to be a dominant investor, there are many suggested action steps for you to follow. If you'll employ these steps you will punch above your weight class. You will have a higher batting average. You will see more deals and buy more deals than you've ever imagined.

Brand is the heart and soul of what Elite Investors are trying to build and preserve. They have a reputation for being likeable, easy to work with, encouraging, and quick to react to opportunities; for showing empathy, teaching similar traits to their staff, fairly compensating and protecting brokers, not re-trading deals, and doing *more* than what they promise and doing it *before* they said they'd do it. Would you expect anything less from someone who is Elite?

The strategies in this book don't seem hard to apply, but they are. It's hard because it requires you to constantly guard your reputation as you're faced with myriad decisions before, during, and after a deal. It seems exhausting to try to befriend dozens of brokers to grow your business. It's hard to monitor your partners and staff to make sure they are maintaining a strong reputation in the market. It's hard to always respond with lightning speed at every step of a deal. It's hard to keep your cool and show empathy in a deal when it seems like the other side is being unrealistic. And it's hard to manage and grow a prosperous real estate investment business while spending enough quality time with family, friends, and personally gratifying endeavors.

There are always twists and turns, high emotions, big dollars, egos, greed, pride, stress, many moving parts, and lots of people involved along the way. It often seems like a miracle when a deal closes, given how many things have to happen nearly perfectly. The reason Elite Investors outperform their competition is because they've built a brand that is inherent to every transaction they do. It's that distinct brand that compels brokers and others to bring them *all* their deals first.

Elite Investors make it easy for a broker to want to do business with them. Elite Investors make brokers look good. Who doesn't want to transact with someone who makes you look good? Make a conscious effort now to begin taking your relationship-building with brokers and other referral parties to a whole new level, and I promise you'll never have to beat the bushes looking for a deal again; they'll find you.

REPUTATION IS THE MOST UNDERRATED SECRET WEAPON FOR COMPLETELY AND CONSISTENTLY DESTROYING THE COMPETITION.

Get serious about your business by mastering a CRM to manage all these relationships. The CRM will make you extremely productive in your business and personal life. Get to know brokers by researching them on social media channels, reading their articles, meeting with them, and talking to them on the phone. It will go a long way when they see you want to know them as human beings. Make an effort to get to know them beyond just buying apartments, and create a deeper motivation on their part to want to do more business with you.

To ensure everyone on your team is staying on track to transact like an Elite Investor, create and consistently update your Love Factor spreadsheet. Your progress in the Love Factor is a direct result of the reputation you are building with brokers. Keep up with surveying each year so you are certain you don't have anyone on the team, including you, who is discouraging brokers from bringing you every deal as soon as possible.

Elite Investors respond rapidly to brokers and to others in the transaction when they are called, emailed, texted, and otherwise contacted about any deals. They respond quickly when making offers, replying to offers, conducting due diligence, and executing closing periods. When brokers and others have to repeatedly wait on an investor, it is a withdrawal from the investor's reputational bank account. When it happens, it can cost them ever even seeing the next opportunity. Every investor is competing with thousands of other investors all over the world for a very few properties that could be potentially purchased. Elite Investors know that brokers have plenty of well-capitalized investors to choose from who will respond quickly and will close.

Elite Investors understand the importance of fairly compensating brokers, both financially and emotionally. They know that when they've helped brokers feel extremely valued for their skills and contributions, brokers are even more motivated to bring more business to them. It's a positive reinforcement loop that will never end, as long as Elite Investors pay brokers fairly and encourage them emotionally. Elite Investors never look for ways to save two cents on a dollar if the penalty is losing major dollars in the future. Elite Investors protect brokers because brokers are their pipeline of new business.

Elite Investors are masters of empathy. They spend time getting to know the participants in a transaction, including their motivation, so they can find commonalities between both parties that will make for smoother transacting and more business in the future. Throughout every interaction, they are considering the other side's position and how any decision will be viewed by everyone else. Elite Investors understand the tremendous multiplying effect, positive or negative, that others spread. They ask themselves what is the right thing to do, not how they can win for themselves. They always check their egos at the door and figure out how they can solve a problem while not just preserving their good reputation but increasing it.

Elite Investors build solid relationships with every broker, as well as each person involved in every deal, but they recognize the value of spending more time cultivating the most productive relationships. Elite Investors are attracted to others who are like themselves, *elite*. Elite Investors know how to spot the best multifamily brokers because those brokers employ the same methods to grow their business that Elite Investors use. Elite Brokers and Elite Investors do a tremendous amount of business together over long careers.

Lastly, Elite Investors focus on being extremely productive when working but leave plenty of time for their family and friends. They've experienced the strains of grinding too hard for too long, and many have recognized it isn't worth it in the end. Most Elite Investors have figured out that spending more time with family, friends, and hobbies actually makes them more relatable to others. A balanced life attracts employees, brokers, and numerous others to them because people like to spend more time in healthy, stress-free relationships. Nobody will remember your investment achievements after your death. More important than money is the quality of the relationships you have with family and friends.

I hope this book opens your eyes to a completely different way of growing your business. The book is based on my observations of actual Elite Investors who are still active today. They are real. I want you to be an Elite Investor. I want to see your unit count grow. I want to see you sell for top dollar. I want to see your business grow faster than you'd ever imagined. Are you ready?

I'd love to connect with you. You can find me on the following social sites, and I encourage you to subscribe to my YouTube channel (BeauKnowsMultifamily), where I show investors how to buy multifamily assets, how to sell them, and how to become a market expert. I post property tours of select listings that YouTube subscribers see first. Also, whether or not you invest in the Florida market, my website is an excellent resource for you to see the reports I run for the markets I cover. Learning your markets in the same way will allow you to more easily respond to opportunities brokers bring you. I can't wait to hear from you.

MY WEBSITE: BeauBeery.com
YOUTUBE: BeauKnowsMultifamily
FACEBOOK: BeauKnowsMultifamily
INSTAGRAM: BeauBeeryGville
LINKEDIN: BeauKnowsMultifamily
TWITTER: BeauBeery

ACKNOWLEDGMENTS

Any first-time author has a preconceived idea that writing a book will not be easy, but most don't know how many other people will be needed to make it successful. A huge thank you to the following people for making my first author experience a positive one.

First and foremost, my real estate coach Blaine Strickland is the driving force behind my getting this book written. He was my motivator to get started. He was my book coach who spent dozens of hours providing game-changing feedback to make the book better and who pointed me to all the sources he used to write two best-selling real estate books of his own. And he has always been my biggest fan.

My father-in-law, Todd Rainsberger, also a commercial real estate broker and author, provided great input on the book that made the read flow smoothly.

My writing coach, Wally Bock, also provided truly outstanding input that opened my eyes to the way readers' minds work as they absorb the text; how to more effectively and efficiently convey ideas so our brains don't miss important concepts.

Lynette Smith is an editor you'll want to call on if you decide to write a book. She makes books readable to all. Elena Reznikova explained how books are designed, which is a fascinating process, and prepared my book for the printing company. Jennifer Reimenshneider, my printer, was patient with me as I learned the process of getting the book from a PDF to print to Amazon.

I'm extremely fortunate through my father-in-law to know and have become friends with Andy Andrews, a *New York Times* best-selling author and in-demand speaker. Andy's wisdom and ability to notice little things that make a big difference in people's lives has been the backbone of the way I conduct business. I'm fortunate he has allowed me to insert a small portion of his work in this book to help the reader understand the power of reputation in the real estate landscape.

To the Elite Investors in my life, you are my heroes. Thank you for not only transacting at an astonishing pace with grace and class, but for showing me how to be a better person to everyone in my professional and personal life. You've made "work" fun for me because it's like getting to hang out with my buddies all day. I wish I could scream to the world who you each are, but I know that isn't your style.

Writing a book takes time away from your family. The most important people I can acknowledge are my wife and kids for allowing me quiet time over a several-months' period while I cranked out the contents of this book. To my wife, Melissa, and our boys, Carson and Gresham, thank you.

ABOUT THE AUTHOR

BEAU BEERY has been in the commercial real estate business in Florida since 1999. He previously earned a Bachelor's degree in Marketing and a Master of Science degree in Real Estate from the University of Florida. Beau also holds the prestigious Certified Commercial Investment Member (CCIM) designation.

Beau began his career in the apartment industry working in property management for three years with Trammell Crow Residential Services (TCRS), one of the largest apartment developers in the country at the time. He learned from the ground floor what it takes to construct, lease, and manage institutional-grade multifamily assets from one of the best in the industry. Beau then worked for nine years as vice president of commercial real estate for AMJ Group Inc., one of North Florida's leading commercial real estate development and investment firms. Beau was responsible for the brokerage and management of the firm's office and retail portfolio, as well as the acquisition of commercial and multifamily investments.

From 2011 thru 2020, Beau teamed up with Todd Rainsberger, a successful commercial Realtor, to acquire an interest in Coldwell Banker Commercial M.M. Parrish Realtors in partnership with the

Parrish family. The firm is a business icon with over 114 years of continuous operation in the local real estate market. It was at this point that Beau decided to specialize in the brokering of multifamily assets. Coldwell Banker Commercial has thousands of agents across 40+ countries. Beau was consistently ranked as the #1 multifamily producer in Florida for the brand and was among the top 5 in the nation every year before starting his own private multifamily brokerage firm in 2021. He is regularly asked to speak at industry conferences and to private companies. Beau also has an ever-growing YouTube channel where he guides viewers on how to buy more multifamily assets, how to sell them, and how to conduct market analysis. His tours of new listings are very entertaining and widely subscribed.

Beau Beery's true passion is being a father to his two boys, Carson and Gresham. Beau has been married to Melissa since 2002. He has many photos showing him with his boys—rock climbing, caving, and whitewater rafting in North Carolina; and also skiing in Utah, swimming, lounging in the hot tub, attending Gator sports, playing in the back yard, boogie-boarding in the surf, and fishing. Beau and Melissa have been avid triathletes, competing in 3–5 races a year, which Beau calls quality time together because they get to travel alone and do what they enjoy. Beau also has an obsessive love for the Porsche 911. He loves to make others smile and laugh, often at his own expense. His father-in-law jests that Beau was born without that part of the brain that allows him to feel embarrassed. Beau's personal motto is, "I live to create unforgettable memories with my wife and kids and bring fun and laughter to others."